# HIDDEN TREASURES

## NORTH YORKSHIRE

Edited by Allison Dowse

First published in Great Britain in 2002 by
*YOUNG WRITERS*
Remus House,
Coltsfoot Drive,
Peterborough, PE2 9JX
Telephone (01733) 890066

All Rights Reserved

*Copyright Contributors 2002*

HB ISBN 0 75433 870 3
SB ISBN 0 75433 871 1

# *FOREWORD*

This year, the Young Writers' Hidden Treasures competition proudly presents a showcase of the best poetic talent from over 72,000 up-and-coming writers nationwide.

Young Writers was established in 1991 and we are still successful, even in today's technologically-led world, in promoting and encouraging the reading and writing of poetry.

The thought, effort, imagination and hard work put into each poem impressed us all, and once again, the task of selecting poems was a difficult one, but nevertheless, an enjoyable experience.

We hope you are as pleased as we are with the final selection and that you and your family continue to be entertained with *Hidden Treasures North Yorkshire* for many years to come.

# *Contents*

        Bethany Dash     1
        Freya Higgins     1

Arkengarthdale CE Primary School
        Peter Sparrow     2
        Sonny Lancaster     2
        Matthew Tommey     3
        Siobhan Smith     3
        Thalia Sparrow     4
        Hannah Hughes     4
        Amy Stubbs     5
        Bethany Stubbs     5
        Daniel Stubbs     6
        Nicholas Dawson     6

Aysgarth School
        Arthur Crawshay     7
        Oliver Lindrup     7
        William Menage     8
        Thomas Lambert     8
        Robert Deane     9
        Rory Lees-Millais     9
        Lawrence Dowson     10
        Christy Furness     10
        George Hasell-McCosh     11
        Andrew Consett     11
        Hugh de Morgan     12
        Oliver Nainby-Luxmoore     12
        Richard Hold     12
        Ben Holmes     13

Birstwith CE Primary School
        Sophie Hodgson     13
        Jessica Umpleby     13
        Robert Umpleby     14
        James Whiteoak     14

| | |
|---|---|
| Katy Mawson | 15 |
| Katie Skinner | 16 |
| Julianne Spence | 16 |
| Cielo Perez | 17 |
| Leo Portal | 18 |
| Tim Robinson | 19 |
| Charlotte Bird | 20 |
| Laura Bartle | 20 |
| Belinda Carney | 21 |
| Sally Grimshaw | 21 |
| Chad Pardoe | 22 |
| Cleone Pardoe | 23 |

**Burnt Yates (Endowed) CE School**

| | |
|---|---|
| Rebecca Leslie | 23 |
| Mariah Redmond | 24 |
| Matthew Morris | 24 |
| James Ugursan | 25 |
| Alex Peter | 25 |
| Elizabeth Swires | 26 |
| Richard Swires | 26 |
| Jemma Bardon | 27 |
| Ben Forse | 27 |
| Amelia Turner | 28 |
| Samantha Crabtree | 28 |

**Cathedral CE Primary School**

| | |
|---|---|
| Scot Bowman | 29 |
| Lauren Gill | 29 |
| Abbey Tufft | 30 |
| Naomi Wass | 30 |
| Victoria Wilson | 31 |
| Emily Bosomworth | 31 |
| Oliver Schofield | 32 |
| Laura Payne | 32 |
| Rachel Ellis | 33 |
| Daniel Coad | 34 |

Eppleby Forcett CE Primary School
|  |  |
| --- | --- |
| Ben Stacey | 34 |
| Austyn Chapman | 35 |
| Leanne Kenyon | 35 |
| Catherine Howson | 36 |
| Eloise Rose | 36 |
| Elizabeth Priestley | 37 |

Gunnerside Methodist Primary School
|  |  |
| --- | --- |
| Laura Calvert | 38 |
| Nigel Waggett | 38 |
| Gail Hunter | 39 |
| Amos Parkes | 39 |
| Susan Whitehead | 40 |
| Carol Whitehead | 40 |
| Eleanor Chadwick | 41 |
| Zoe Wearmouth | 41 |
| Matthew Calvert | 42 |
| Andrew Calvert & Joe Sammells | 42 |
| William Porter | 43 |
| Steven Coates | 43 |
| Avril Hunter | 44 |
| Benjamin Hall | 44 |
| Emma Hopwood | 45 |

Holy Trinity CE Junior School
|  |  |
| --- | --- |
| Stephen Ingall-Tombs | 45 |
| Nicola Blair | 46 |

Hookstone Chase Primary School
|  |  |
| --- | --- |
| Thomas Hardy | 46 |
| Mia Slinger | 46 |
| Scott Richardson | 47 |
| George Hirst | 47 |
| Joanne Allcock | 48 |
| Stacey Worrall | 48 |
| Connor Holroyd | 48 |
| Lewis Edwards | 49 |

| | |
|---|---|
| Thomas Flynn | 49 |
| Kirsty Hunter | 49 |
| Chloe Knight | 50 |
| Kirsty Hunter | 50 |
| Joe McCann | 50 |
| Robert Ellis | 51 |
| Amie Tipling | 51 |
| Mathew Wills | 52 |
| Melanie Saville | 52 |
| Adam Hodgson | 52 |
| Ian McKenna | 53 |
| Alex Lister | 53 |
| Brynmor Powell | 54 |
| Chris Stones | 54 |
| Rebecca Sharples | 54 |
| Sam Slade-Nelson | 55 |
| Samuel Taylor | 55 |
| Ryan Maples | 55 |
| Abigail Holbrough | 56 |
| Lauren Frazer | 56 |
| Lisa Thomas | 57 |
| Daniel McDonald | 57 |
| Hannah Rose Virden | 57 |
| Chloë Brookes | 58 |
| Elliot Bowman | 58 |
| Nikita Wilkinson | 58 |
| Craig Kennedy | 59 |
| Ashley Knapton-Smith | 59 |
| James Wright | 60 |
| Amy Rollings | 60 |
| Charlotte Ulman | 60 |
| Thomas King | 61 |
| George Shilton | 61 |

**Hutton Rudby Primary School**

| | |
|---|---|
| Jo Pye | 62 |
| Jennifer Nelson | 63 |
| Lela Young | 63 |

|  |  |
|---|---|
| Andrew Porter | 64 |
| Emma Stokes | 64 |
| Jonathan Grey | 65 |
| Spencer Phillips | 66 |
| Holly Smeaton | 66 |
| Bekki Rowe | 67 |
| Eva Barnes | 68 |
| Daniel Puttick | 68 |
| William Ruff | 69 |
| Hannah Whittingham | 70 |
| Grace Seller | 70 |
| Melissa Darwent | 71 |
| Emma Charlton | 72 |
| Sam Malone | 72 |
| Charlotte Bennington | 73 |
| Kate Simpson | 74 |
| Martin Lane | 74 |
| Stephanie Williams | 75 |
| Becky Innes | 76 |
| Thomas Ruff | 76 |
| James Walton | 77 |

Kirkby Fleetham CE School

|  |  |
|---|---|
| Ashlee Sharp | 78 |
| Duncan Mason | 79 |
| Joshua Atkinson | 80 |
| Katy Gill | 80 |
| Sam Toothill | 81 |
| Rachel Tiplady | 81 |
| Harriet Henderson | 82 |
| Lois Jermyn | 82 |

Langcliffe Primary School

|  |  |
|---|---|
| David Leighton | 83 |
| Thomas Lee | 84 |
| Daniel Newhouse | 84 |
| Charlotte Jeffrey | 85 |

| | |
|---|---|
| Imogen Pilling | 85 |
| Alexandra Jeffrey | 86 |

Le Cateau Community School

| | |
|---|---|
| Hayden Goodwin | 86 |
| Kimberley Mossman | 87 |
| Rebecca Hall | 87 |
| Chantelle Lyal | 88 |
| Shannon-Lea Alder | 88 |
| Apryl Kennedy | 89 |
| Charlotte Mott | 90 |
| Marc Bullimore | 90 |
| Abigail Mortimer | 91 |
| Tayler Froehling | 92 |
| Christopher Stewart | 92 |
| Zack Eddie | 93 |

Longman's Hill CP School

| | |
|---|---|
| Leanne Smith | 93 |
| Adam Smith | 94 |
| Sophie-Jade Marshall | 94 |
| Amelia Vickers | 95 |
| Sam Bruce | 95 |
| Jamie Hambrecht | 96 |
| Joshua Gibbon | 96 |
| Natalie Hambrecht | 97 |
| Nathan Parker | 98 |
| Holly Ness | 98 |
| Mathew Weston | 99 |
| Amy Williams | 100 |
| Lee Moore | 100 |
| Lauren Littlewood | 101 |
| Jake Marshall | 102 |
| Courtney Graves | 102 |
| Kirsten MacGregor | 103 |
| Emma Cook | 104 |
| Luke Swithenbank | 104 |
| Luke Scott | 105 |

| | |
|---|---|
| Michelle Scott | 106 |
| Denika Yorke | 106 |
| Gordon Wilkinson | 107 |
| Fay Horn | 107 |
| Geraint Thomas | 108 |
| Katherine Wright | 108 |

Markington CE Primary School

| | |
|---|---|
| Anna Stockil | 109 |
| Christie Johnson | 109 |
| Daniel Flanagan | 110 |
| Anya Johnson | 110 |
| Daniel Wilberforce | 111 |
| Callum Otley | 111 |
| Katie Bates | 112 |
| Andrew Schofield | 112 |
| Emma Foster | 113 |

North & South Cowton Primary School

| | |
|---|---|
| Zoe Wolstenholme | 114 |
| Chloe Edwards | 114 |
| Laura Turner | 115 |
| Katie Wilson | 116 |
| Richard Ozelton | 116 |
| Kate Harrison | 117 |
| Joshua Riley-Fox | 117 |
| Sarah Adamson | 118 |
| Rebecca Howell | 119 |
| Martin Clark | 119 |
| Nicola Wilson | 120 |
| Simon Nicholson | 120 |
| Yasmin Welham | 121 |
| Louise Pearson | 121 |
| Abby Weighell | 122 |
| Dexter Turner | 122 |
| James Donaldson | 123 |
| Daisy Shaw | 123 |

| | |
|---|---|
| Raegan Shaw | 124 |
| Bethany Wilson | 124 |

**Romanby Primary School**

| | |
|---|---|
| Stacey Robson | 125 |
| Ellis Hayes | 125 |
| Matthew Codd | 126 |
| Jamie Kirby | 126 |
| Sebastian Rab | 127 |
| Richard Hounsome | 128 |
| Grace Kirk | 128 |
| James Lacy | 129 |
| Joe Clarkson | 130 |

**St Cuthbert's Primary School, Pateley Bridge**

| | |
|---|---|
| Lindsay Walker | 130 |

**St Hilda's RC Primary School, Whitby**

| | |
|---|---|
| Jasmine Briggs | 131 |
| Magnus McAuley | 132 |
| Josie Wilkinson | 132 |
| Marcia Kipling | 133 |
| Francesca Roe | 133 |
| Francis Clark | 133 |
| Frances Wright | 134 |
| Amy Pearson | 134 |
| Frances Cairns | 135 |
| Kirstie Lloyd | 135 |
| Rikki Roach | 136 |

**St Martin's CE Aided Primary School, Scarborough**

| | |
|---|---|
| James Howe | 136 |
| Richard Walker | 137 |
| Jonathan Corrie | 137 |
| Ben Smith | 138 |
| Robert Squire | 138 |
| Annie O'Sullivan | 139 |
| Rosie O'Sullivan | 140 |

|  |  |
|---|---|
| James Aitchison | 141 |
| Samuel Tindall | 141 |
| Robert Mead | 142 |
| Charlotte Harrison | 143 |

St Nicholas CE Primary School, Ripon
|  |  |
|---|---|
| Alicia Salt | 144 |
| Steven Durrans | 145 |
| Sam Watkins | 146 |
| Ben Ambler | 147 |
| Emma Scott | 147 |
| Jessie Perry | 148 |

St Wilfrid's RC Primary School, York
|  |  |
|---|---|
| Stefania Finch | 148 |
| Isobella Turnell | 149 |
| Keziah J Brookes | 150 |
| David King | 150 |
| Hannah Jackson | 151 |
| Nicole Zannikos | 151 |
| Andy Baker | 152 |

Settrington All Saints CE Primary School
|  |  |
|---|---|
| Nicole Vogwill | 152 |
| Rebecca Stubbings | 153 |
| Samantha Marwood | 154 |
| Beth Nicholson | 154 |
| Jade Hoggard | 155 |
| Rosie Buckland | 156 |

Thorpe Willoughby CP School
|  |  |
|---|---|
| Tasha Lawrance | 157 |
| Dale Holt | 158 |
| Stephen Dean | 158 |
| Cameron Robertson | 159 |
| Natalie Carse | 160 |
| Adam Carse | 160 |
| Katie Matthews | 161 |

| | |
|---|---|
| Rebecca Yould | 162 |
| Sam Grinsill | 162 |
| Stacey Welbourn | 163 |
| Leanne Walker | 164 |
| William McVittie | 164 |
| Adam Taylor | 165 |
| Tom Rich | 166 |
| Jack Greenwood | 166 |
| Hayley Pallett | 167 |
| Christopher Allen | 168 |
| Danielle Amos | 168 |
| Jennifer Raechel Carter | 169 |
| Jake Lount | 170 |
| Louise Jackson | 171 |

Threshfield Primary School

| | |
|---|---|
| Natasha Cahill | 171 |
| Harry Bullough | 172 |
| Emma Ferguson | 172 |
| Rosanna Booth | 173 |
| Monica Yeadon | 174 |
| Ruth Anderson | 174 |

Wilberfoss CE Primary School

| | |
|---|---|
| Simon Barnes | 175 |
| Samuel Blunt | 176 |
| Amy Pack | 176 |
| Georgina Warren-Porter | 177 |
| Alex Mercer | 177 |
| Charlton Wilson | 178 |
| Courtney Rossiter | 178 |
| Andrew Healey | 179 |
| Megan Hugill | 179 |
| Sarah Veitch | 180 |
| Nikol Bishell-Wells | 180 |
| Georgina Pattison | 180 |
| Daniel Poole | 181 |
| Hannah Green | 181 |

| | |
|---|---|
| Francesca Bennet | 182 |
| Harry Hughes | 182 |
| Katherine Ames-Ettridge | 183 |
| Elliot Etherington | 183 |
| Alice Bean | 184 |
| Esme Dawber | 184 |
| Rachael Cotgrave | 185 |
| Rosie Bentley | 185 |
| Katie Last | 186 |
| Serena Leach | 186 |
| Robyn Childe | 187 |
| Amy Gover | 188 |
| Katrina Graves | 188 |
| Alice Sey | 189 |
| Jake Gilbertson | 189 |
| Rachel Hopwood | 190 |
| Rebecca Bowe | 190 |
| Josh Barrett | 191 |
| Catriona Burns | 191 |
| Alex Nattrass | 192 |
| Rachel Hudson | 192 |
| Zoe Robinson | 193 |
| Victoria Gomersall | 193 |
| David Laverack | 194 |
| Samuel Vale | 194 |
| Katie Bentley | 195 |
| Ashley Oliver-Scott | 195 |
| Zoe Frost | 196 |
| Joseph Mellanby | 196 |
| Jessica Fleming | 197 |
| Matthew Poole | 198 |
| Caroline Harrow | 198 |
| Lois Gilbertson | 198 |
| Mark Cundle | 199 |
| Rachel Alexander-Pratt | 199 |
| Rebecca McFetridge | 200 |
| Sophie Ollerenshaw | 200 |
| Emily Childe | 201 |

| | |
|---|---|
| James Hopwood | 201 |
| Alex Gurnell | 202 |
| Jason Nattrass | 202 |
| Andreas Symeonides | 203 |
| Christopher Fenn | 203 |
| Ryan Downes | 204 |
| Tom Connell | 204 |
| Jemma Bayes | 205 |
| Tom Hughes | 205 |
| Ashley Cattle | 206 |
| Alice Ames Ettridge | 206 |
| Jade Taylor | 207 |
| Jade Watson | 207 |
| Elliott Murphy | 208 |
| Lawrence Crawford | 208 |
| Sarah Hartas | 208 |
| Emma Knutton | 209 |
| Amanda Smillie | 209 |
| Robert Pickard | 210 |

Woodfield Community Primary School

| | |
|---|---|
| Rory Megginson | 210 |
| Andrew Lewis | 211 |
| Sasha Buck | 212 |
| Ian Porter | 213 |
| Matthew Button | 214 |
| Thomas Claxton | 214 |
| Emily Rowe | 215 |
| Jack Clayton | 215 |
| Bethanie Sturdy, Kirsty Owen & Charlotte Voakes | 216 |
| Carlene Smith | 217 |
| Alex Lenton & Shaun Deeming | 218 |
| Emily Webster | 219 |
| Daniel Johnson, Tim Newell & Kelly Gilmour | 220 |
| Daniel Andrews-Turner | 221 |

| | |
|---|---|
| Natalie Healey, Hollie Forge & Leah Mercer | 222 |
| Kelly McQuigg | 222 |
| Natalie Robinson-Bramley | 223 |
| Emma Buckee | 224 |
| Mark Teggin, Michael Groves & Billy Wood | 224 |
| Luke Foggin, Sarah Jenner & Nicola Evers | 225 |
| Lorraine Mazza | 226 |
| Jonathan Binns, Thomas Steventon & George Morton | 227 |
| Damien Oliver & Jade Moffatt | 228 |
| Bethany Aitken | 229 |

*The Poems*

# RIDDLES

I sleep all the time
I have cuddly fur
Dogs say woof
But I say purr.
I come in black,
White and more
Surely you have
Seen me before.
I will claw your curtains
Your carpet and mat
You must know by now
That I am a cat.

I live on a planet
Of rock and gas
My skin is the colour
Of dead, crispy grass.
I'll suck your brain
If I want your knowledge
Then bury your body
In a forbidden forest.
If I don't kill you
I'll at least give you scars
I am an alien
From planet Mars.

*Bethany Dash (10)*

# SNOW

Flakes drift side to side
Children throw freezing snowballs
Fat snowmen shiver.

*Freya Higgins (7)*

## GOING TO EGYPT

I'm going to Egypt
Where all the special treasures are
I'm going to explore in the desert
I'm going to explore for treasure
Where are the tombs?

I don't know
I will have to find my way
I'm going to see beautiful, amazing, shining treasures

What I found
A trap door
Which revealed to me a magnificent
Ancient tomb

Down, down, down I went
I found a sealed door
A seal saying Tutankhamun
Thousands of treasures were sparkling like diamonds
Thousands of memories of old Egypt
Here we go back
With all the treasures.

*Peter Sparrow (9)*
*Arkengarthdale CE Primary School*


## THE DREAMCATCHER

I take it everywhere with me
I don't know where I would be without it
It gives me good dreams
I don't know what I would do if the feathers got lost
It's so beautiful during the night
It makes me feel happy.

*Sonny Lancaster (7)*
*Arkengarthdale CE Primary School*

## TREASURES OF EGYPT

Think of all the treasures,
All of the lovely pleasures,
The tombs of Tutankhamun, Nefertiti, Akhenaten, Rameses,
In a model guard's hands there were some keys,
The keys led to a burial chamber,
The corridor couldn't be stranger,
At the end of the corridor they came to a room
A sudden voice said, 'You've sealed your doom!'
But the treasures were beautiful,
None of them were dull,
They found a gorgeous, golden gate
But by the time they wanted to leave,
It was far too late!

*Matthew Tommey (9)*
*Arkengarthdale CE Primary School*


## TREASURE BOX

I've got a little treasure box
Hidden somewhere
But it doesn't hide in the cupboard
Or on the chair
It goes everywhere with me
It is really hard to see
It's got happy memories and sad ones too
It's also got wishes and dreams
Warm and special thoughts
Shall I tell you where they are
And tell you where to find them?
You will have to cut me up
Because they're in my precious mind.

*Siobhan Smith (10)*
*Arkengarthdale CE Primary School*

## MY TREASURES

I have a box of treasures
I keep it to myself
It's always there when I want it
I peep in there when I'm feeling sad
But you can't peep, it's only me
I keep my memories inside it
Gifts and special things
My wishes are always there
My rings and jewellery are there
Pottery too
My gifts which I want each night
They're always there when I want them
I have a box of treasures
I keep it to myself.

*Thalia Sparrow  (7)*
*Arkengarthdale CE Primary School*


## MY TREASURE

My teddy is the best.
I cuddle him every night.
He never runs away from me.
He's never out of sight.
I take him everywhere I go.
We never stay apart.
He's not very good at maths
But he's a work of art.
My teddy is the best.
I put him in my bed at night
And cuddle him so, so tight.
*Goodnight teddy!*

*Hannah Hughes  (7)*
*Arkengarthdale CE Primary School*

## MY TREASURES

I've got a soft teddy,
I've got a big panda,
I've got a big, soft teddy and panda.

I've got a bright daffodil,
I've got a little plant,
I've got a little, bright daffodil.

I've got a computer CD,
It's about amazing maths,
I've got an amazing maths CD.

I've got a dull lighthouse,
It always flashes,
I've got a dull, flashing lighthouse.

All these things are my treasures,
They all stay with me,
They will never leave my side.

*Amy Stubbs (10)*
*Arkengarthdale CE Primary School*


## MY HIDDEN TREASURES

I have a treasure box
It's full of special things
It's got earrings that glitter like gold
It's got crowns that glitter like silver
It's got rings that shine like the sun
It's got necklaces like chains
Those are my special things.

*Bethany Stubbs (8)*
*Arkengarthdale CE Primary School*

## MY TREASURES

M ums and dads,
Y oung brothers and sisters.

T eddies and toys,
R elics and medals,
E nvironment and nature,
A nimals and dreams,
S pecial gifts and memories,
U nicorns and fantasy,
R ivers and oceans,
E nchantment and magic,
S aviours and friendship.

*Daniel Stubbs (10)*
*Arkengarthdale CE Primary School*


## EGYPT

I'm in the sandy desert
I just don't know what I'll do
Maybe I'll go find a tomb
Or go and see the Nile again
Well now I'm going for sure
I don't know what I'll do
I know, I'll go and see a tomb
The glint of gold, bits of silver
Food bags in a hole in the wall
Models and sculptures
These are all that I saw today.

*Nicholas Dawson (7)*
*Arkengarthdale CE Primary School*

## HIDDEN TREASURE

H undreds of miles into the deep.
I bet the treasure's in a cavern.
D igging holes in the sand, might find it.
D eep, deep down.
E vening is coming, must hurry.
N ow rocks ahead.

T reasure, lots and lots of treasure.
R iches and jewels.
E verywhere are sparkling gems.
A nd magic stones sparkling and flashing.
S panish galleons bursting with gold.
U reka I'm rich.
R iches of every sort
E ven kings crowns and swords.

*Arthur Crawshay (10)*
*Aysgarth School*


## HIDDEN TREASURE

There are rubies, sapphires and gems,
All locked up in a box.
Silver and gold and strange tales to be told,
All locked up in a box.
Down, down at the bottom of the ocean,
Sweets and drinks and potions and lotions,
All locked up in a box.
Hidden away with all its treasures,
Down at the bottom of the ocean,
Emeralds and mysteries never to be found,
Treacherous creatures in the sea,
All guarding this one big box.

*Oliver Lindrup (10)*
*Aysgarth School*

## Untitled

H eaving through the everlasting desert
I nsecure and dull
D etermined to find and dangerous to get to
D esperate and excited, hopefully its not full
E xpensive jewels, worthless tools
N ever bothers me.

T reacherous creatures
R eptiles and mammals
E ating and breeding
A t last I know
S ustained and survived
U nderneath a cave
R uthless and brave
E vermore there is no secret any more.

*William Menage (10)*
*Aysgarth School*


## Hidden Treasure

I walked into some caves on a mountain top,
I went in by myself,
I could not see anything in the rocks
Until I noticed something brown and small,
It was under a big rock in this kind of hall,
I went to have a look, it was a match case,
I opened it up with great delight,
I saw some tickets with my name on
To the cricket world cup.
Maybe it was my birthday present as it was coming up.
That is how I found my treasure.

*Thomas Lambert (10)*
*Aysgarth School*

## TREASURES HIDDEN

T reats and surprises for you to find,
R ubies and sapphires glowing brightly
E ven a ticket to Disneyland Paris
A forest full of jewellery
S uper gems hidden in rabbit holes
U nder the sea there are many surprises
R eady for people to crack wide open
E verywhere you go watch for hidden treasures
S ilver and gold under the sea.

H appy smiles and faces when people find treasure,
I n the ocean there are every kind of goods
D ig deep and you will find
D elicious surprises for you to eat and keep
E ven an old dinosaur bone
N ear the shore.

*Robert Deane (10)*
*Aysgarth School*


## HIDDEN TREASURE

T rekking onward rough and ragged, rocks and rivers all around
R ambling up a great big hill with all my friends,
E ye! What's that! I'd seen something glowing in the light,
A gily I clambered to the spot, nothing at all
S itting down on a rock I heard a squeak, it was my seat!
U nfamiliar glints and twinkles, lots of shapes and cold, hard feelings,
R iches! Of all sorts, diamonds, rubies, you can name them all,
E ventually I realised I had found all the money I would ever need!

*Rory Lees-Millais (11)*
*Aysgarth School*

## HIDDEN TREASURES

Hidden under a blinking, big slab,
I saw only worms and bugs, nothing bad,
But then with a surprise I saw a lump hidden under all the bugs,
That's all that needed to get me going,
I started digging with my hands and stones,
I was revealing something very big or to me it seemed to be,
I was tugging and pulling at the lock
Then I realised I should examine the box
Look at the box, I thought what a box,
The lock I could just hit it with a rock
And I would be in like an octopus
I saw two jewels, they were diamonds
Both as big as golf balls,
Next day I hid them safe and sound
Somewhere it will never be found.

*Lawrence Dowson (11)*
*Aysgarth School*


## HIDDEN TREASURE

T ingling, shimmering in the light ray
R iches of crowns and pounds
E meralds, rubies of gleaming red
A mongst weeds and sunlight beams
S harks guarding and fish darting and twinkling
U nder the deep blue sea
R uins of wrecks and bodies from the dead
E verywhere gold and silver is scattered on the bare seabed.

*Christy Furness (11)*
*Aysgarth School*

## SMUGGLERS' CAVES

I was going to explore the smugglers' caves,
On the shore by the sea, Granny had said
I was crawling through the wet and slime,
Of the largest cave of all.
When suddenly I saw something up ahead,
A black, rusty box locked up tight
The wood was rotten though, easy to break
But inside there was nothing like you've ever seen before;
Deep blue sapphires, rubies and pearls,
Golden crowns and thousands of pounds,
All shimmering like fire,
It was riches beyond expense.

*George Hasell-McCosh (11)*
*Aysgarth School*


## NEW BIKE

H idden beneath the straw
I deas buzzing through my head
'D on't guess,' said Mum
D ad said, 'Don't go looking for it again'
E ven through I've found it
N ow I've got to wait

B irthday coming soon
I can't wait
K ate says, 'It's a pitchfork!'
E ven she has got it wrong.

*Andrew Consett (11)*
*Aysgarth School*

## OCTOPUSSY

T urning, twisting at the bottom of the sea
R ed, beady eyes
E nergy ready to be used
A ngry from the crime
S ecret treasure has been stolen
U nder the watchful eyes of the octopus
R eady to attack any that come to claim it
E nraged and ready to tear anything apart.

*Hugh de Morgan (10)*
*Aysgarth School*


## HIDDEN TREASURE

H idden deep in the sea
I n a giant oyster
D eep inside there lies a giant pearl
D ragging it out
E ngaging the sun
N ow it looks as good as good can be, almost like a crown.

*Oliver Nainby-Luxmoore (11)*
*Aysgarth School*


## HIDDEN TREASURES

Hidden deep away in the banks of Egypt
Lay a ship in the big, black sea
With a treasure big and bold
A pearl with an everlasting glow
A mystery never to be told.

*Richard Hold (11)*
*Aysgarth School*

## UNTITLED

T rembling by the
R aging current
E ating at the chest
A fter dusk octopus guards it from the dead
S houting and shattering from the boats above
U nderneath the muddy sand are the
R emains of the
E verlasting gold.

*Ben Holmes (10)*
*Aysgarth School*

## SOPHIE

S ophie snail sailed away from the spiky, hot sun
O ver a big waterfall that made Sophie snail all cold
P itter-patter the water fell on Sophie snail
'H elp,' Sophie snail cried.
'I am falling down a waterfall.'
E nd of Sophie snail.

*Sophie Hodgson (9)*
*Birstwith CE Primary School*

## THE SNOWMAN

He has my dad's old hat and a carrot for a nose.
His eyes are neither blue or brown, but only some black coal.
His mouth is always strangely shaped, usually with coal
His tummy is very round, we patted it all day.
But he does not have any legs or toes to wiggle around
But he does not get cold like us but he hates the heat.

*Jessica Umpleby (8)*
*Birstwith CE Primary School*

## FLYING WEATHER

We took off while the wind was calm,
And it did not do us any harm.
We flew up very, very high,
And we went up through the clouds and sky.

We weaved through the weather and met
An immense cloud like a massive net.
We came to rain lashing quite hard,
It looked to be acting like a guard.

At last we came to sunshine bright,
Just the opposite to the dark night.
Next came snow, a bit of a shame,
But who must take the horrible blame?

Over the blue Pacific sea,
It was calm. We were singing with glee.
Flying over the desert hot,
It was very like a steaming pot.

Coming into land in Britain,
I realised I had lost a mitten.
When we were coming and losing height,
It was foggy just like after night.

***Robert Umpleby (11)***
***Birstwith CE Primary School***


## MUMMIES

Guarded by a curse of doom,
Hidden away in a cold, dark tomb,
The archaeologist ignores the curse of doom
As he enters the cold, dark tomb.

Down the stairs spreading rust and dust
It's darker, cold,
It's cold, so very
So cold, very cold . . .

*James Whiteoak (10)*
*Birstwith CE Primary School*

## MY POEM

I want to win this competition
And writing a poem is my mission.
My poem isn't even fit for the bin
So I definitely won't win!

Poems are my weak spot,
My poem will probably rot.
Because I've just spilt my drink
While I was having a think.

Now my poem will not win
As my mother placed it in the bin.
I'll have to write it out again
Where did I put my pen?

Brain I've got to write a poem
And it normally all goes wrong.
I'm not really good at poems,
But I could write you a song.

No, I've got to write a poem!

*Katy Mawson (11)*
*Birstwith CE Primary School*

## DOGS

Dogs jump,
    Dogs howl
Some even bite and growl.

Dogs are playful,
    Dogs are not
It doesn't matter a lot.

Dogs are soft,
    Dogs are tough
Some are really, really rough.

Dogs guard things,
    Dogs don't
Some dogs won't.

Dogs lie down,
    Dogs heel
Sometimes they don't seem very real.

Dogs prance,
    Dogs dance
Some beg for their food.

Dogs lick,
    Dogs rule
But I think dogs are cool.

*Katie Skinner (9)*
*Birstwith CE Primary School*


## HORSIE

As we ride around the field
Galloping faster and faster
I pull the reins and crack my whip
I show her I am master.

When I am in the stable
I put on her saddle
I polish her bridle
While I'm sat at my old table.

*Julianne Spence (9)*
*Birstwith CE Primary School*

## THE HORSE

Hoof kicker,
Ear flicker,
Mane flower,
Quick goer,
Eye blinker,
Shoe clinker,
Cute looker,
Lip pucker,
Show jumper,
Door bumper,
Good glider,
Speedy rider,
Nose muzzler,
Hand nuzzler,
Tail flicker,
Face licker,
Hay sucker,
Strong bucker,
Slow eater,
Nothing to beater,
Fast runner,
What a stunner!

*Cielo Perez (10)*
*Birstwith CE Primary School*

## THE MONSTER ALPHABET

A is for *Anter* with poisonous jaws.
B is for *Biter* with bleeding claws.
C is for *Clatter* who bites if you don't work.
D is for *Dragular* who does nothing but lurk.
E is for *Ekker* with big, stomping feet.
F is for *Fighter* who'll turn you to wheat.
G is for *Ghosty* he'll give you a fright.
H is for *Hinkular* on Saturday night.
I is for *Iper* who will sneak up behind.
J is for *Jackalog* certainly not kind.
K is for *Kartan* who rips you apart.
L is for *Lumpy* damaging a cart.
M is for *Moose* who will chase the goose.
N is for *Naughty* with a bad chocolate mousse.
O is for *Orange* who will knock down the church.
P is for *Piggy Wink* with a squeal and lurch.
Q is for *Quiet* who'll creep to your room.
R is for *Rough Bag* lying in tomb.
S is for *Strong* who'll squeeze out your blood.
T is for *Teethy* who will eat you with mud.
U is for *Under* just under your bed.
V is for *Viper* who will bite off your head.
W is for *Wellington* who will roar in your ear.
X is for *X-ray* who'll gnaw till you won't hear.
Y is for *Yucky* who'll spit in your food.
Z is for *Zippy* in a greedy mood.

***Leo Portal (10)***
***Birstwith CE Primary School***

## THE TIGER

The tiger decides to go a-hunting
Beware the animals of the forest
The mighty beast, the king of cats
Is going to come a-hunting.

It slinks through the grass,
Its eyes fixed on the buffalo.
The mighty cat gets closer, it bares its fangs for all to see,
The beast looks round, it sees the tiger.

The tiger's feet like metal springs
Push twenty stone clean off the ground
Onto the back of the buffalo,
Bringing it down with a crash.

The tiger paws the beast.
The buffalo is a feast.
He lets out an almighty roar
That comes out of his vast jaw.

More tigers are a-coming
To feed off his prey.
They all take a hearty bite
Before another animal comes into sight.

The black and gold animals
Swish their tails round.
They do not make a sound
When they're on the prowl.

*Tim Robinson (10)*
*Birstwith CE Primary School*

## SCHOOL DINNERS

Green, mouldy slime
That's supposed to be grave.
Some sort of grime
Which looks kind of navy.

The crumb-covered fishes
With carrots that are black.
And all I wish is
That I don't have tooth plaque.

The disgusting jelly,
With custard gone cold.
Puts shivers in my belly
If you eat it all you're bold.

*Charlotte Bird (10)*
***Birstwith CE Primary School***


## FROGS

Frogs jump, frogs leap,
In a bundle, in a heap.
The greatest divers in the world,
Bent up all day, aren't their legs curled?
Slimy body, scaly skin,
His throat makes an awful din.
They smell like eggs all day,
All day his legs are in the way.
His legs! His legs!

*Laura Bartle (8)*
***Birstwith CE Primary School***

## I Don't Care

I walked across the meadows . . . dusty,
    But I don't care
I fell over the tree roots,
    But I don't care.
Fell down a big, black hole,
    But I don't care.
Got attacked by a big blackbird,
    But I don't care.
Uurrghh, stuck in thick, squelchy mud,
    But I don't care.
Fell in dirty, rocky, brown waters,
    But I don't care.
And I did all this on my way to a friend's house
    But it was worth it.

*Belinda Carney (10)*
*Birstwith CE Primary School*


## My Dog

My dog is daft and funny
He plays with my fat bunny
He plays with me and runs with me
All day long!
My dog is dumb and dumber,
He plays with me
He bounces up and pounces up
All day long!

*Sally Grimshaw (9)*
*Birstwith CE Primary School*

## THE RIDDLE

A stealthy fleet of galleons
Silhouetted against the dark waters
Edging stealthily,
The shadows slink.

What are these vile things
That lie on shadowy waters?
Scaled backs, they do have,
We see them in the light.

They do not fly
Yet move so quick
Brazened in the blackness,
Though murky in the light.

Snicker-snack like a farmer's
Scythe cutting through the corn
Not alive, but from an egg are
Their children born.

Their feet are webbed
Though claws protrude,
Through the sagging skin.
They do eat stones but
Don't eat bones to help with what's
Within.

Can you solve this puzzle
Like a riddle of the sphinx?
Do you know what the creature
With the scaled back is?
The jaws that make a snicker-snack
Big jaws
No paws
*Sharp claws!*

**Chad Pardoe (11)**
**Birstwith CE Primary School**

## THE BLIZZARD

Frightening, cold snow,
Roaring round me,
As I lie on the floor,
Panting with fright.

Cold goose bumps all over me,
I try and get up
But the wind knocks me over
With its sharp, cutting blows.

Now what will come?
More danger?
I hope not!
But the wind gets up again
Raging around me.

I call for help,
But the snow is too hard.
No one can hear me.
I fall down feeling as if I'm
*Dead!*

***Cleone Pardoe (8)***
***Birstwith CE Primary School***


## NIGHT-TIME

When night falls and the light becomes dark
And the shadows all leap into action
We go to sleep and we don't take a peep
At what's going on alongside us
We sleep through the noise that's going on outside
But still we do not stir
For we are far, far away in dreamland and that you just can't change.

***Rebecca Leslie (9)***
***Burnt Yates (Endowed) CE School***

## MEMORIES IN A BOX

One day I find a jewelled box inside another box,
Deep inside my box of ambitions, inside my untidy closet.
I open it.
I'm now floating over a roller coaster.
I'm looking down on my family, I don't think they notice me,
But they seem to be having great fun.
I remember that we went to a theme park and had a good time.
Once I'd remembered that
I vanished and was now over a beach.
I was swimming with my sister.
That was the time we went to the beach for half a month.
Poof! I was not at a park playing with my friends,
It was summer holidays and we were so happy.
Bang! I was dancing at my aunt's after-wedding ceremony
And it was so exciting I couldn't sleep.
I kept tripping over my dress it was so long.
There was a flash, I was home,
And I thought, good or bad I've friends and family to take care of me.

*Mariah Redmond (9)*
***Burnt Yates (Endowed) CE School***

## IN MY TREASURE BOX

I will put in my treasure box . . .
A bag of shiny, colourful rubies.
I will put in my treasure box . . .
Thousands of sparkling gems and crystals
Dripping with beautiful colours from the rainbow.
And I will put in my box . . .
A bag of hundreds and hundreds of golden gold
Bouncing and twirling like a pencil writing neatly
On a piece of paper.

*Matthew Morris (9)*
***Burnt Yates (Endowed) CE School***

## THE LOST TREASURE

I will put in my treasure box:
All the beautiful pearls in the world and the biggest beetle.
I will put the Atlantic Ocean in a corner of the box
A Viking sword and spear
All of Venice and its boats
In another corner shining stars bright and light
A hot rainforest and all the birds
Like blackbirds and blue tits and hidden treasure underwater.

I will put in my treasure box:
All the motorbikes in the world
Dinosaur's egg the size of a shoe,
Big, bad wolf and the three little pigs
The biggest calculator in the world
So I can add all the numbers in the world
The biggest and *fastest* roller coaster ride in the world
So every morning before school I can have fun on it.

*James Ugursan (9)*
*Burnt Yates (Endowed) CE School*


## MY TREASURES

I found in a box, treasures of the world:
A ruby with heat as strong as the sun.
The Amazon rainforest with different coloured snakes.
A night sky filled with stars that shine like diamonds.
Waves that wash shells a hundred miles.
The sweet song of a blue tit in the morning.
The love of my mum in my heart.
A wand with powers as strong as God.
A tooth made out of sapphire, diamond and emerald.
A place where your wishes come true.

*Alex Peter (8)*
*Burnt Yates (Endowed) CE School*

## MY TREASURE

I will find in the box:
A queen with a nucleus of pearls the size of stones.
And a family with treasures from around the world.

I will find in the box:
A mermaid with a tail of diamonds and golden hair
As long as a country.

I will find in the box:
A song that is sung by a thousand birds.
A cat that is a hundred different colours.

I will find in the box:
A book that never ends.
And a dinosaur's egg.

I will put in the box:
My family, my relations and my friends.
These are my greatest treasures.

*Elizabeth Swires (10)*
*Burnt Yates (Endowed) CE School*


## FINDING THINGS

I can find a treasure in a cave, my sister and a game.
I can find my friend in a ship.
I can find a rubber in a volcano.
I can find a book full of spells, and a potion in the ocean.
I can find the pet squad, and the Romans.
I can find 49 jewels in my bag,
And a cup full of water that lasts forever.
I can find a computer game under the bed.
I will find them soon!

*Richard Swires (7)*
*Burnt Yates (Endowed) CE School*

## THE BOLT OF LIGHTNING

I saw a bolt of lightning
Flashing across the sky.
Then it came to a sudden halt,
It stared at me.

I could see the way it glared at me.
It looked scary and evil.

Although I could not see
It was smiling at me,
I was afraid and worried.

It came up to me,
I better not touch the window
Otherwise it will shock me
But it had no shock inside.

I did not see
But it's just a lonely lightning bolt.

*Jemma Bardon (10)*
*Burnt Yates (Endowed) CE School*


## MY TREASURE

C   omes with wires
O   bviously safe
M   ade of glass and plastic
P   lugged into a socket
U   ses modern technology
T   aking electricity from a station
E   conomy can be good or bad
R   eally special to me.

*Ben Forse (8)*
*Burnt Yates (Endowed) CE School*

## ELEPHANT GRAVE

Elephants live in groups of families
They have an old elephant in the pack
She is called the matriarch
The matriarch has led the other elephants to feeding grounds.
When an elephant dies the others grieve
And groan
Sometimes they pick up the bones and stroke them.
Elephants never forget
Dead or alive they both have ivory
They are becoming extinct
We all have to do our bit to save the elephants.

*Amelia Turner (10)*
*Burnt Yates (Endowed) CE School*


## MY MEMORIES

Memories are my treasures hidden
Away at the back of my head,
Like the first lamb of spring,
The first tweet of a baby bluebird,
The crack of a chicken's shell,
And the smells of the morning grass.

Like the sounds of a river,
The roaring of a tractor,
The splashing of a whale
And the shining of the silvery moon.

*Samantha Crabtree (10)*
*Burnt Yates (Endowed) CE School*

## FIVE DAYS OF SKATEBOARDING

Day One:    Attempt to ollie
Fall over backwards
What a wally.

Day Two:    Try to kick-flip
Aaaaah! Gonna slip
Oh no, fat lip.

Day Three:    Skate a mini ramp
Stop halfway down
Get cramp.

Day Four:    Attempt to grind
Fall off the rail
Losing my mind.

Day Five:    Perhaps it's not for me,
With a bruised back, a fat lip, cramp and a sore knee,
Now I've switched on the TV.

*Scot Bowman (10)*
*Cathedral CE Primary School*


## MICE

I think mice are rather nice
Their tails are long, their faces are small,
They haven't any chins at all.
Their ears are pink, their teeth are white,
They run about the house at night.
They nibble things they shouldn't touch
And no one seems to like them much.
But I think mice are rather nice.

*Lauren Gill (11)*
*Cathedral CE Primary School*

## SEASONS

First is winter, cold and dark
No one in the abandoned park
Jack Frost is near
Can you hear
The wind's whispering in your ear.

The next is Spring
Listen to the birds sing
Spring flowers grow
And the farmers sow
The corn, wheat and vegetables.

Then it's summer, bright and hot
No need for stew cooking in a pot
Holidays are here
Because summer is back.

Last is autumn
Bright, crunchy leaves
Fall off all the trees
All the children go please, please, please
To play in the leaves.

*Abbey Tufft (8)*
*Cathedral CE Primary School*

## ROBOTS

R   oma is a robot,
O   ff she goes to do your jobs,
B   ernard's house first,
O   ff to the next,
T   hen she's back again with my tea,
S   he's a good, little robot my *Roma*.

*Naomi Wass (10)*
*Cathedral CE Primary School*

## TREASURE HUNT

There's treasure under the sea I see,
One day a pirate said to me,
'How do you know?'
He gave a wink,
Because, he said, 'I saw it sink.'

'Let's take a boat and have a look,
But don't forget your fishing hook,
We could be rich, just you and me,'
'But I told my mum I'd be home for tea.'

But in our boat we *did* set sail,
And then we saw a giant whale,
'Hello,' the whale said to me,
'I've found some treasure, come and see,
Put on your goggles and open your eyes,
I'll show you where the treasure lies.'

We found the treasure,
Oh what a pleasure,
We took it up and had a look,
It nearly snapped our fishing hook,
Our adventure is over on the sea,
So now I'm going back for tea.

*Victoria Wilson (9)*
*Cathedral CE Primary School*

## SNOW

S now is great
N ow let's throw snowballs
O h no, the snow is melting
W ow, it's gone already.

*Emily Bosomworth (8)*
*Cathedral CE Primary School*

## BACK TO SCHOOL

Here we go again,
Back to school to see a fool running around the playground,
The bell has gone
With a dong.
In we go,
Some quite slow,
We do some English,
We do some maths,
Whoopee, this afternoon's PE.
It's play time now, let's go on out
What fun it is to play in the sun.
The bell has gone,
I've had some fun
The Head is coming,
Red in the face.
Marching, marching at quite a pace,
Trouble, trouble, what have we done?
Nothing, nothing, he marched right on!
In we go to do more work!

*Oliver Schofield (10)*
*Cathedral CE Primary School*


## ANIMAL POEM

Hamsters are like owls who sleep in the day.
When darkness falls they come out to play.

Poor, cold puppies in the street.
Bring them in and give them heat.

Fluffy, white cats miaow and purr.
They keep warm with their lovely, cosy fur.

Parrots squeak and squawk all day long.
Sometimes they sing a lovely song.

Most kinds of animals are very nice.
The ones I don't like are mice.

*Laura Payne (8)*
*Cathedral CE Primary School*


## FAIRIES

The tooth fairy:
When the tooth fairies come
They are so quiet
They take your tooth away
They leave a pound under your pillow
For you to find next day.

The birthday fairy:
The birthday fairy
Is just as nice
She leaves you lots of presents
But only if you have been good
Maybe six or seven.

The Christmas fairy:
Santa needs someone to assist
The Christmas fairy is on his list
He calls to her don't delay
Because soon it will be Christmas Day
On Christmas Day everyone has fun
Because of what she has done.

*Rachel Ellis (8)*
*Cathedral CE Primary School*

## A MAN CALLED DAN

There was an old man called Dan,
Who lived in a small caravan,
One day he played cricket,
And got a great wicket,
That clever, old cricketing man.

*Daniel Coad (10)*
*Cathedral CE Primary School*


## THE GORGON

There was once a boy called John
He always seemed to get along
With beasties, bugs and silly things
Things that crawl and things with wings.

Once his dad told John
About a beast called the Gorgon
So off he set without a word
He couldn't believe what he heard.

Roar and crash!
Bang and smash!
So he picked up his sword
And stabbed its tummy
And the Gorgon said,
'Yummy, yummy, you look scrummy.'

He removed his sword
The Gorgon was no more.
How he killed it I can't say
So now it's safe to play.

*Ben Stacey (9)*
*Eppleby Forcett CE Primary School*

## Fog

The fog is pretty thick
And everyone is scared
To go in the fog.
The fog is so cold
And everywhere frozen
Then old grandpa comes
And slips on the ice.

Everyone is cold
And children play in the cold fog.
Everyone is slipping and sliding
On the thick ice.
Mice squeal when cats are out
But the cats are scared
When the fog's about.

*Austyn Chapman (11)*
*Eppleby Forcett CE Primary School*

## Snow

Snow is falling
    soft and fluffy
Covering everything
    white and bright
Children playing
    slip and slide
            skate
                    skid
                          slip
                                slide
Snow falls
    white and bright.

*Leanne Kenyon (8)*
*Eppleby Forcett CE Primary School*

## IF I WERE REINCARNATED?

If I were reincarnated
A hippo I would be.
Not a swimming, slippery fish
Roaming the deep, blue sea.
Not a bouncy kangaroo
Leaping up high,
Not a sharp-eyed eagle
Skimming in the sky.
Not a powerful lion
Fierce, big and strong.
Not an upside-down bat
Staying up all night long.
Not a slow slow-worm
Digging underground.
Nor a quiet, quiet mouse
Not making a sound.

A hippo I would be
Lumbering in the river
Eating fish all day long
Singing the muddy hippo song.
The river horse is for me
Just me and my friend Henrietta.
Life as a hippo would be so much better.

*Catherine Howson (10)*
*Eppleby Forcett CE Primary School*

## LIGHTNING STRIKES TWICE

The sky cracked open wide
The electric mist crept down.
It touched my face, goodbye
I thought, as I slumped down.
I am going to Heaven.

But I saw before me my friends
And got up again.
But the sky cracked open once more
And the mist came down.

Then I screamed the scream
That no one heard.

I am gone.

*Eloise Rose (9)*
*Eppleby Forcett CE Primary School*

## THE CAT

Creeping in the shadows
Slinking on the roof
Landing lightly on his feet
The nine lives have proof.

A mouse is never missed
The cat coils like a spring
Paws the mouse skilfully
The tiny body gets a fling.

Purring at the front doors
He's kicked back on the street
Hissing with deep hatred
With nothing nice to eat.

Feeding on the scraps
He is king of the alleyways
He tries to get a loving home
But the dustbin is where he stays.

*Elizabeth Priestley (10)*
*Eppleby Forcett CE Primary School*

## TEN LITTLE CARS

10 little cars speeding in a line,
one went down the street, then there were nine.
9 little cars whizzing because they're late,
one crashed into a lorry, then there were eight.
8 little cars zooming up to Heaven,
one got stuck, then there were seven.
7 little cars scoffing pick 'n' mix,
one went down the lane, then there were six.
6 little cars trying to stay alive,
one had a big crash, then there were five.
5 little cars trying not to snore,
but one did, then there were four.
4 little cars, one couldn't see,
it was obviously blind, then there were three.
3 little cars one ate a shoe,
he chewed it all up, then there were two.
2 little cars one ate a scone,
then there was one.
1 little car with a driver like a hero,
went too fast, then there was zero.

*Laura Calvert (9)*
*Gunnerside Methodist Primary School*


## MY PET

K  ittens are one of my favourite animals and I have one
I   ts name is Marmalade
T  he kitten's mum is called Sally
T  he kitten is a ginger cat
E  very day I feed it, morning and night
N  igel is its owner.

*Nigel Waggett (10)*
*Gunnerside Methodist Primary School*

## LEAD MINES

The lead mines were bleak,
chilly,
dirty,
dusty
and dark.

Knitting sticks went clicky-clack, clickety-clack
As the men trudged to work.

Barren now, but fill of depressed people
then,
cold,
wintry,
bare,
lifeless,
plain.

Sweaty men slowly pick their
Way out of the grim lead mines
To clean, fresh air.

*Gail Hunter (10)*
*Gunnerside Methodist Primary School*


## MY BEST FRIEND

My best friend has three white paws
One white leg and a pink licky tongue.
He has two long ears
And two droopy eyes.
He likes his dinner and he likes his tea
*But*
Best of all he likes me!

*Amos Parkes (9)*
*Gunnerside Methodist Primary School*

## RIVER SWALE

R acing gently past the eroding bank.
I nterestingly she calmly winds herself through the valley
V arious rocks get deposited onto her stony banks.
E xploding like a big firework.
R ippling smoothly down the stream.

S plashing frantically as the rain comes pouring down into the river.
W ater thrashing and crashing over the rocks.
A ll the rivers shimmering or bursting run into the sea.
L ightly she falls down the waterfall.
E roding trees and banks, falling into the fast-flowing river.

*Susan Whitehead (11)*
*Gunnerside Methodist Primary School*




## RIVER SWALE

R ivers can go softly or overflowing
I go to the river sometimes,
V ery quickly the river goes when it is in a flood,
E ven if it is raining it might not flood,
R oaring, thrashing, bashing, crashing,

S tony beds on the bottom of the water,
W ashing the fish while they are swimming,
A t the top there are floating leaves,
L ight flashes onto it,
E nd of the day.

The river might be at the sea by now.

*Carol Whitehead (8)*
*Gunnerside Methodist Primary School*

## RIVER SWALE

R aging through and through the river races downstream.
I cy-cold water thrashes past with flashing waves.
V ast and rumbling, the river explodes over the river bank.
E roding, the river rages tearing rocks and boulders with it.
R ippling, the river foams over the shimmering stones.

S wiftly, the rushing river transports branches and boulders.
W aving and spurting it thrashes and crashes through,
A ching, the river moans and groans while it charges through.
L iving like a sea serpent curving and meandering.
E ating away at the river bed.

*Eleanor Chadwick (10)*
*Gunnerside Methodist Primary School*

## RIVER SWALE

R umbling and roaring as it goes past.
I ron coloured water comes streaming fast.
V eins in the river come tumbling down.
E agerly down the flashing river.
R ippling down makes the water shiver.

S himmering, rustling, moving down.
W ater is rushing to the town.
A lmost knocking down the wall.
L eaving a gentle, calm wave.
E rosion over, a very wet grave.

*Zoe Wearmouth (10)*
*Gunnerside Methodist Primary School*

## WHY THERE'S A SPLODGE?

Why's there a splodge on the road?
Tell me
Why's there a splodge on the road?

An alien came down to Earth
He didn't look, he didn't care
People started to stand and stare

Why's there a splodge on the road
Tell me
Why's there a splodge on the road?

He didn't stop, he didn't care
He crossed the road
A truck came along with a very large load

Why's there a splodge on the road?
Tell me
Why's there a splodge on the road?

He didn't listen, he didn't care
The lorry load flew up in the air
And the lorry squashed the alien!
That's why there's a splodge on the road!

*Matthew Calvert (8)*
*Gunnerside Methodist Primary School*


## ALWAYS WEAR YOUR HELMET

Cars zooming
Lorries chugging
Always wear your helmet.

Tractors roaring
Mopeds are boring
But always wear your helmet.

Cycling along the road
Flying down the hill
*Crash!*
He didn't wear his helmet.

*Andrew Calvert (11) & Joe Sammells (10)*
*Gunnerside Methodist Primary School*

## RIVER SWALE

The river rumbling as the boulders crash
And splash on their way down the river.

Roaring river rushing and dirty coloured
Water taking the stones and fallen trees down the river.

Ripping the earth from the side of the river
Reaching land and trees down the river.

*William Porter (9)*
*Gunnerside Methodist Primary School*

## THE RIVER SWALE

The river is like thunder
The river is bashing and smashing
The side overflowing
Into the field
Crashing walls down
Trees too
Are coming down the river.

*Steven Coates (8)*
*Gunnerside Methodist Primary School*

### RIVER SWALE

She is calm then mad,
Depositing everything she had.
She foams with rage,
As if in a cage.

She rushes by,
People say, 'Oh my!'
She is bursting with stones,
That want to be home.

She is meandering by,
Not caring why.
As she ripples,
She turns to a trickle.

*Avril Hunter (10)*
*Gunnerside Methodist Primary School*

### THE RIVER SWALE

Watch the crashing, thrashing river
Go raging down the stream
Bashing crinkled stones
Watch the thundering, bursting river
Going flashing down the valley
Look at it go raging
Thumping in the river
Can you see it roaring,
Overflowing?
See it rushing down the bendy stream
Look at the dirty colour rustling in the river
Watch the smashing, racing river go raging.

*Benjamin Hall (9)*
*Gunnerside Methodist Primary School*

## Bells

The world is full of different bells.
There are animal bells, like cow bells.
There are safety bells, like fire bells.
There are festive bells for Christmas and for Santa's sleigh.
Special occasions bells for weddings and services.
There are flower bells like bluebells and harebells.
There are useful bells like doorbells and shop bells.
Then there are school bells for play time, dinner and
The favourite with children
*The going home bell!*
So the world is full of bells.
Ding
    Dong
        Ding
            Dong
                Ding
                    Dong.

***Emma Hopwood (10)***
***Gunnerside Methodist Primary School***


## Two Best Friends On Their Journey To Bethlehem

The sand dances with pleasant mirth
The sun slept like a hovering fire.
The womb whimpered with the sunlight within.
The donkey chattered to the whispering wind,
They discussed the beauty of the child,
The friends he would make
The enemies he would gain,
And his death for love.
They could see the event would be the light of the world.

***Stephen Ingall-Tombs (11)***
***Holy Trinity CE Junior School***

## THE GHOST SHIP

She sat silently there
Proud and tall,
Whispering to the still ocean.
Mist surrounded her and the moon hung high above.

She cried out, wounded by her loneliness,
Darkness dwelled beside the silent, solemn ship
Moans echoed through the night.

As dawn came, she slipped into a silent dream,
The ghost ship gone.

*Nicola Blair (10)*
*Holy Trinity CE Junior School*


## HAPPINESS

Happiness is making things out of materials
It is a time of joy
And a time you can laugh
Happiness is a joyful time
It is the time of your life
And you can enjoy yourself
But most of all happiness is being with my family.

*Thomas Hardy (9)*
*Hookstone Chase Primary School*


## RECIPE FOR WINTER

Take a drink of hot chocolate while you are inside.
Add the snowball fights.
Mix with friends and family
Stir in the cake.

Sprinkle with frost.
Decorate with trees covered in snow.
Leave the season standing.
Serve at Christmas.

*Mia Slinger (9)*
*Hookstone Chase Primary School*

## ANGER

Anger is a flaming fire
And it is the lightning of the storm inside you.
It is the darkness of the midnight sky.
Anger is the exploding of the volcano
And it is the giving of pain.
Anger is the destruction of the body,
But most of all anger is never heard
Until you unleash it.

*Scott Richardson (10)*
*Hookstone Chase Primary School*

## HAPPINESS IS . . .

Happiness is when I have lots of friends
And when I play on my skateboard
It is when I go to my friend's house
Happiness is when I get new toys
And when I go to school
Happiness is when I'm playing on the PlayStation
But most of all happiness is being me.

*George Hirst (9)*
*Hookstone Chase Primary School*

## RECIPE FOR SUMMER

Take a day picking fruits
Add ice cream
Mix with going on holidays
Stir in suntan cream
Sprinkle on cold drinks
Decorate with sunshine
Leave to relax.

*Joanne Allcock (9)*
*Hookstone Chase Primary School*


## RECIPE FOR SUMMER

Take long, hot summer's days
Add suntan lotion
Mix with hot holidays
Stir in cold ice cream
Sprinkle on summer sunshine
Decorate with the sunshine
Leave to cool down.

*Stacey Worrall (9)*
*Hookstone Chase Primary School*


## RECIPE FOR WINTER

Take animals hibernating
Add sparkling frost
Stir in shorter days
Mix with colder days
Decorate with snowmen
Leave to freeze
Serve with Christmas presents.

*Connor Holroyd (9)*
*Hookstone Chase Primary School*

## RECIPE FOR SUMMER

Take hot, sunny days
Add suntan lotion
Mix with cool drinks
Stir in cold showers
Sprinkle on holidays
Leave to cool down
Serve on the beach.

*Lewis Edwards (9)*
*Hookstone Chase Primary School*

## RECIPE FOR AUTUMN

Take crisp, flaky leaves
Add ripe, ripe fruit
Mix with tiny hedgehogs
Stir in cooler weather
Decorate with dew
Leave until Hallowe'en
Serve with blackberries.

*Thomas Flynn (9)*
*Hookstone Chase Primary School*

## RECIPE FOR WINTER

Take hibernation
Add sleeping flowers
Mix with bare trees
Stir in snowflakes
Sprinkle on white blankets over the land
Leave to freeze
Serve in warm beds.

*Kirsty Hunter (9)*
*Hookstone Chase Primary School*

## RECIPE FOR WINTER

Take a frosty, cold day
Add some floating snowflakes
Mix with crunchy, crisp leaves
Stir in snowball fights
Sprinkle on a coat of snow
Decorate with a nice, warm fire
Leave to freeze
Serve at Christmas time.

*Chloe Knight (9)*
*Hookstone Chase Primary School*


## RECIPE FOR SUMMER

Take beach balls
Add pretty flowers
Mix with ice creams
Stir in sunbathing
Sprinkle with hot days
Decorate with smiling faces
Leave to burn
Serve with suntan lotion.

*Kirsty Hunter (9)*
*Hookstone Chase Primary School*


## RECIPE FOR SUMMER

Take boiling hot weather,
Add picnics in the garden.
Mix with lots of ice cream,
Stir in a nice walk in the park.

Sprinkle in a nice, relaxing holiday,
Decorate with hot summer sun.
Leave to cool down,
Serve in the garden.

*Joe McCann (9)*
*Hookstone Chase Primary School*


## RECIPE FOR SUMMER

Take barbecues
Add long evenings
Mix with nice, cold ice
Stir in ice cream
Sprinkle on green leaves
Decorate with holidays abroad
Leave to cool down on a beach
Serve in the garden.

*Robert Ellis (9)*
*Hookstone Chase Primary School*


## RECIPE FOR SUMMER

Take hot summer weather
Add suntan cream
Mix with cool ice cream
Stir in hot, sandy beaches
Sprinkle on hot sunshine
Decorate with cool milkshake
Leave to cool down
Serve in the garden.

*Amie Tipling (9)*
*Hookstone Chase Primary School*

## RECIPE FOR SUMMER

Take hot summer days
Add the ice cream on the shore
Mix with suntan lotion
Stir in the beautiful, hot sun
Sprinkle on the long days
Decorate with light, sunny days
Leave to warm up
Serve on the beach.

*Mathew Wills (8)*
*Hookstone Chase Primary School*


## RECIPE FOR SUMMER

Take hot, sunny weather
Add suntan cream
Mix with cold ice cream
Stir in hot, sunny beaches
Sprinkle on wonderful sunshine
Decorate with summer
Leave to cool down
Serve in the garden.

*Melanie Saville (9)*
*Hookstone Chase Primary School*


## RECIPE FOR SUMMER

Take lots of summer days
Add lots of fun
Mix with the warm sun
Stir in cool ice cream

Sprinkle on sand from the beach
Decorate with sea waves
Leave to cool down
Serve with sun-ripened tomatoes.

*Adam Hodgson (9)*
*Hookstone Chase Primary School*

## RECIPE FOR SUMMER

Take the hot summer sun
Add deck chairs on sand
Mix with ice cream to cool you down
Sprinkle suntan lotion
Sprinkle on holidays
Decorate with swimming trunks
Leave to cool down
Serve on the boat.

*Ian McKenna (9)*
*Hookstone Chase Primary School*

## RECIPE FOR SUMMER

Take the boiling-hot weather
Add holidays
Mix with cold water to cool you down
Stir in buttercups and daisies
Sprinkle on the wonderful sunshine
Decorate with shiny sparkle from the sun
Leave to cool down
Serve with sun ripened fruit.

*Alex Lister (9)*
*Hookstone Chase Primary School*

## RECIPE FOR WINTER

Take short days
Add lots of cold weather
Mix with hanging icicles
Stir in hot chocolate
Sprinkle on snowflakes
Decorate with silver frost
Leave to freeze
Serve by hot, blazing fires.

*Brynmor Powell (8)*
*Hookstone Chase Primary School*

## RECIPE FOR SUMMER

Take hot days
Add ice cream
Mix with yellow and blue
Stir in the pool
Sprinkle on long days
Decorate with sunlight
Leave to warm up
Serve on the beach.

*Chris Stones (8)*
*Hookstone Chase Primary School*

## THE FIREWORKS

I see bonfires and rockets glistening
I smell hot dogs sizzling
I hear fireworks loudly banging
I touch sparklers like rain
I eat hot dogs that are gorgeous.

*Rebecca Sharples (10)*
*Hookstone Chase Primary School*

## HALLOWE'EN

It's dark as dark, it's Hallowe'en!
Exciting treats to eat.
Up and down the streets
Trick or treat,
Don't get tricked, just say treat.
It's not a nightmare, it's only me.
Witches, ghouls and ghosts we are.
Don't be scared, it's Hallowe'en!

*Sam Slade-Nelson (9)*
*Hookstone Chase Primary School*

## HALLOWE'EN

On this dark and scary night
Get ready to jump and have a fright.
You never know who you'll meet
A ghost, a witch or a trick or treat
Pumpkins glowing like a fire,
A knock at the door
It's . . . a vampire!

*Samuel Taylor (9)*
*Hookstone Chase Primary School*

## FEAR IS . . .

Fear is ghosts!
And it is being afraid.
Fear is a dark forest at night
And it is being lost on a dark night.
Fear is vicious
But most of all fear is just plain fright!

*Ryan Maples (9)*
*Hookstone Chase Primary School*

## HALLOWE'EN NIGHT

Silent and dark but for the moon,
The witches will be out very soon.
It's the night of Hallowe'en.
And if you look carefully all sorts can be seen.
There's vampires, ghosts, cats and witches,
Out on this night to gather some riches.
The witches with warts as ugly as can be,
The vampires and ghosts running round free,
The pumpkins so pretty are bright like the stars,
I'm sure that the aliens can see us from Mars.
We're out trick or treating,
All our friends we are meeting
But we don't know who they are!
They could be from a land afar.
Round the corner comes a mummy,
I thought he looked very funny.
We had a great night it was ever so spooky,
We got lots of goodies and plenty of money!

*Abigail Holbrough (9)*
*Hookstone Chase Primary School*


## HAPPINESS IS . . .

Happiness is when I eat melted chocolate
And when Leeds United win the cup
It is when I go home and tea's on the table
Happiness is when people are nice to me
And when I get involved with things
Happiness is when I have company
But most of all happiness is joy and friendship.

*Lauren Frazer (9)*
*Hookstone Chase Primary School*

## HAPPINESS IS . . .

Happiness is getting up on a Saturday morning
Saying I don't have to go to school.
And playing on my street with my friends.
It is nice eating lots and lots of yummy chocolate.
Happiness is having lots of friends at school
And when my mum doesn't wake me up in time for school.
Happiness is when a friend comes to play at my house from school
But most of all it's spending time with my family and friends.

*Lisa Thomas (10)*
*Hookstone Chase Primary School*


## SADNESS

Sadness is when you're grumpy and bitty
And you're feeling sick inside.
It's like your teeth are all so gritty.
Sadness is when you're being cut or grazed by nettles
But most of all it is the bad things happening in the world.

*Daniel McDonald (9)*
*Hookstone Chase Primary School*


## ANGER IS . . .

Anger is a horrible feeling inside you,
It's like lightning on a stormy night,
Anger is fireworks bursting in your stomach,
It's like a volcano erupting inside you,
But worst of all anger makes you feel sad.

*Hannah Rose Virden (9)*
*Hookstone Chase Primary School*

## HALLOWE'EN

H aunted by the sacrifices of the past
A spellbinding scream.
L augh in the face of danger.
L ively spirits dance around you,
O bservers unseen, lurking in the shadows.
W itches and warlocks wind up the living and wither away.
E very light dims and flickers,
E choes of screams everywhere
N asty ghosts glint in the dark.

*Chloë Brookes (10)*
*Hookstone Chase Primary School*


## FIREWORKS

F ireworks
I love them to death
R aying the sky with such bright lights
E nding darkness in the sky
W atching them light up the air
O h we love them bursting in colourful ways
R oar go rockets up in the air
K ings of the sky
S et the crowd alight with joy.

*Elliot Bowman (10)*
*Hookstone Chase Primary School*


## HALLOWE'EN

Hallowe'en time is here once more
Someone's knocking at the door.
Everyone's a scary sight,
Pumpkin faces all alight.

Witches, ghosts and spooks about
'Trick or treat!' the kids all shout.
Children's bags full of sweets
Hallowe'en - a night for treats!

*Nikita Wilkinson (10)*
*Hookstone Chase Primary School*


## HALLOWE'EN

H allowe'en is an exciting night,
A ll the ghouls come out to fright.
L isten closely and you may hear them
L aughing at the tricks they play.
O range pumpkins with scary faces,
W itches flying through the streets,
E vening time when it gets dark,
E erie noises, screams and howls,
N ight passes and they disappear to return next
*Hallowe'en*

*Craig Kennedy (9)*
*Hookstone Chase Primary School*


## I SEE

B alls of flames I see go up through the sky.
O ver all the people I see it open like a bud.
N othing is so beautiful as a Catherine wheel,
F ire of the bonfire flickers on and off like a light.
I see the loud ones open like spiders legs,
R ings of sparklers the children make,
E nd of the firework show.

*Ashley Knapton-Smith (9)*
*Hookstone Chase Primary School*

## HAPPINESS IS . . .

Happiness is going on holiday
It is swimming in a deep and warm pool
And it is playing at the seaside on a hot day.
Happiness is the biggest slice of chocolate fudge cake
And Leeds United when they win.
Happiness is playing with your friends
But most of all happiness is being with your family.

*James Wright (10)*
*Hookstone Chase Primary School*


## HAPPINESS IS . . .

Happiness is a warm time when I am with my family,
And also when I have a new toy like some new Beanie babies.
Happiness is when your imagination comes alive,
But most of all happiness is being with my friends.

*Amy Rollings (10)*
*Hookstone Chase Primary School*


## HAPPINESS IS . . .

Happiness is having lots of friends,
And having good luck!
Happiness is laughing with your friends and family
But most of all happiness is having a fun time.

*Charlotte Ulman (9)*
*Hookstone Chase Primary School*

## VLAD THE BAD

Vlad the Bad is back again
And he's not feeling any shame.
He's ready to do a terrible thing
He wants the world, he wants to be king.
King of the world that is his dream,
People will cry, people will scream.
He wants destruction,
He wants demolition,
He wants the whole planet
So he's on this great mission.
Don't go near him he is insane
Vlad the Bad is back again!

*Thomas King  (9)*
*Hookstone Chase Primary School*


## HAPPINESS IS . . .

Happiness is playing on my Game Boy
And playing with my friends,
It's a joyful and happy time
Happiness is being with my friends and family
And playing on my PlayStation 2
Happiness is eating chocolate
But most of all happiness is seeing fireworks
Exploding in the sky.

*George Shilton  (9)*
*Hookstone Chase Primary School*

## ODE TO AUTUMN

Autumn is here.
Ochre coloured leaves pirouette downwards drifting like a graceful
dancer, swiftly landing, softly on her toes.
I see prickly, brown hedgehogs scurrying and snuffling around
searching for fat, juicy, hairy spiders, slimy, black slugs and
adventurous snails, leaving behind only their silvery trail.
Patchwork fields scattered about,
seem to glow golden in the early morning sun.
The corn stalks sway gently,
carefully protecting their precious, golden jewels.
The lovely scent of fresh autumn flowers
are all different shades and colours.
They line pretty gardens and dense forests.
An abundance of crispy, rosy-red apples ripening in the autumn sun,
hanging from a gnarled tree.
Shimmering, glinting spiders' webs
sparkle with tiny pearl-like dewdrops,
showing up the dainty design of the elegant web.
At a large horse chestnut tree, small and large children gather,
collecting mahogany conkers, to later battle with.
Their spiky shells crack just a little bit so you can just see inside.
A sunset paints its way across the sky with pinks, reds and oranges.
Winter pulls up the old orangy-brown carpet,
and puts down a perfectly white one.
Bleak days now follow
autumn is gone.

*Jo Pye (11)*
*Hutton Rudby Primary School*

## AWAKENING OF THE MORNING

The moon wakes from her deep sleep yawning over all
The glinting diamonds sparkle as they slowly fade away.
The sun paints over the blackness with pink, blue, red,
gold, white and magenta.

The sleepy robin awakes from his nest and starts its song,
followed by the rest of the birds all lead by him.

The sun reaches out its fingers and slowly hauls itself up
in place of the moon.

Its pale, warm glow beams down on the ground,
waking the plants and flowers.

Slowly, the lights in houses flick on and more people
get up to the colourful morning.

*Jennifer Nelson (10)*
*Hutton Rudby Primary School*


## THE AWAKING OF THE MORN

The last whisky fox of the night slinks home to its isolated den.
Proud cocks crow like rich kings of the morning land.
A woken tree stretches its gnarled limbs as if it has been
aroused from a powerful trance.
Evening stars flicker like broken fairy lights,
disappearing into the misty morn.
The blazing sun, which is a great ball of gold,
crimson, scarlet and yellow draws and paints a wonderful picture
of the universe's palette, positioned in the daybreak sky.
Night has been defeated.
Morning has hardly begun.

*Lela Young (10)*
*Hutton Rudby Primary School*

## ON A MOONLIT NIGHT

As I entered the misty forest, I glanced back at the deserted town
shining in the tranquil moonlight.
As I started to descend, down a very muddy path, I felt myself
being engulfed by the murky air.
A musty smell began to filter through my nostrils.
I began to veer off the sludgy path, I came to a small clearing
where I stared at the twilight sky.
I gazed up at the sparkling jewels, encrusted in the silky air,
then a myriad points of light shone upon the ferny ground.
The foots of the old trees glittered peacefully in the light.
I looked up at the ancient and gnarled, withered old trees,
like dark, silhouetted figures, waving sinisterly in the night sky.
I watched silently as a majestic owl splayed out its feathers
which had been draped around its solitary body.
A bushy squirrel bounded off, up a gnarled oak,
its tail like a fibre optic light.
A lumbering badger squeezes out of its sett,
its noir coloured hair, shimmering in the silver light.
I turned back and started to head home, it was midnight.
As I got to the forest mouth I thought of the bulbous eyes of the owl,
the cumbersome badger, the majestic trees
and the magic of a moonlit night.

*Andrew Porter (10)*
*Hutton Rudby Primary School*


## BONFIRE

I can see a fierce saffron beast rapidly gaining strength
Its golden teeth consume all its dinner in its red-hot mouth.
It breathes out a gasp of fire as it swallows its favourite food.

It spits out flames that die and turn into blood.
I see it trying to escape the breeze that makes it shiver.
It gives me a fierce look and it concentrates just on me.

Rain starts pelting down on it then it dies down a little bit.
It starts to suffer and screams out all its breath.
It has one flame left and as the one last raindrop falls,
It hits it and kills it.

*Emma Stokes (11)*
*Hutton Rudby Primary School*


## ON A MOONLIT NIGHT

I sit on the tranquil bank of a luminous stream with glimmering water.
I gaze, entranced at an ancient oak crouched over like a respected elder.
The distant echo of a bell could be heard chiming through the air
marking the still existence of the placid town.
I lay on the fleecing heather on top of the lofty mountains, the only
thing killing my solitude was the screech of a mystical creature.
As I stare upwards on my downy bed of springy heather, I fall
into the gentle grip of joyous wonder as I scrutinize at the myriad
points of light in the voluminous night sky.
I wander into my misty forest, jumping in and out of the pools of light
that have been carelessly thrown around.
Moonbeams shoot around the trees, rippling in pools of tears.
I sit on the tranquil bank of a luminous stream with glimmering water,
the sun is coming.
I fall back, swimming in my night's memories.
The moon has been lost to the important, colossal sun,
rising to its expectant child, Earth.
The cute spark of the stars are caught in a vast, beautiful fishing net,
and towed away to fathomless distances.
The sun silhouettes my old oak tree.
It hurls itself at my lofty hill, painting it with magical colours.
It bounces off my soft heather.
It lights up the way in my misty forest.
I will never forget the strange magnificence of the serene night.

*Jonathan Grey (11)*
*Hutton Rudby Primary School*

## ON A MOONLIT NIGHT

As I enter the forest I see the bent, crooked trees
Leaning over me and the crumpled and crisp leaves
Scattered all over the ground.
The mysterious night grabbing all light in its reach.
The night sky shimmering like glitter in the air.

The moon is glowing brightly at me.
As I am looking into space, I see the endless twilight gone.
When I look into the heavens, I see the sky is silhouetted with colour.
Again I look into space, only to see a shooting star shining brightly.

I hear an owl hooting softly through the darkness of the night.
Foxes rustling amongst the crunchy leaves.
A badger sniffing around the old trees.
In the dark I see nothing except the bright moon.

As I walk through the woods, I hear birds cheeping and chirping.
The first bird of the day appears.
A great ball of fire spreading its light and heat.
The night has been beaten again by the sun.

*Spencer Phillips (10)*
*Hutton Rudby Primary School*


## MORNING MAKER

The horizon begins rolling back the black carpet, and painting;
Pink, purple, cream, gold and blue.
The silhouetted moon fades away scared of daylight,
To unravel his black carpet on someone else.
The old, gnarled tree tap taps on the small window
Of the old, red house.

An early blackbird awakens,
As the old owl goes home to the old, gnarled tree.
A small hedgehog scuttles into a pile of leaves.
The dewdrops on the flowers glisten.
The sun glides up slowly and reaches his long fingers down.
The puffy clouds glide into place.
The morning is made.

*Holly Smeaton (11)*
*Hutton Rudby Primary School*


## SUMMER REMEMBERED

A winter's morning closes in with his frost cloak
Draped along the ground.
The grass struggles through, fighting the cold air,
A barn owl settles down, as a blackbird awakes.
An early morning factory lorry groans, waking up from its sleep,
Children sleep soundlessly in their warm beds.
The stars fade, like the reflective eyes of a cat.

A robin chirps cheerfully in a nearby tree,
Then paints his background with reds, pinks and golds.
The blackbird is awake competing against the sound of the robin.
A cat prowls on the frost-covered ground searching for his dinner.

A child stirs ready to awake from her sleep,
The sun pushes in advancing on the night, like a lion ready to pounce.
The child awakes like the blackbird,
The cattle graze in the dewy fields.
The newborn sun is ready for his day.

*Bekki Rowe (11)*
*Hutton Rudby Primary School*

## AUTUMN DAYS

The clear, crystal, frosted snowdrops melt
and trickle down my red, chilly nose.
A black, spotted quilt takes over the world
when I close my blue, gleaming eyes.
The glittered moon shines upon the wet,
muddy fields.
You can see patchwork as the farmers cut
the golden corn.
A prickly, cold hedgehog settles down in the
wavy, ochre leaves.
The glittering moon goes down as the golden, fiery
sun creeps up.
Crimson leaves crisp up in a flaky ball.
Gorgeous robins sing as every leaf touches the frosty ground.
Bleak birds are all in solitary brown.
Colourful birds perch on a thick log.
The sun has gone and I have gone,
but my memories have not.
The dark has come back.
The first snowflake floats to the ground.
Winter is here, autumn will come again.

*Eva Barnes (10)*
*Hutton Rudby Primary School*


## THE LISTENERS

He staggers along the dusty road tiring with every pace,
Yet he still goes on throughout the night
As if to win a race.
He steps up and opens the door and calls,
'Is anyone there?'
He hears no answer, yet carries on
Then feels the wind run through his hair.

He hears the storm outside the house
Before the front door closes,
He starts to clamber up the stairs
While a phantom appears and the traveller screams
Whilst the listeners watch and snigger
The traveller faints, turns white in the face
While one decides to pull the trigger!

*Daniel Puttick (11)*
*Hutton Rudby Primary School*


## THE WARM AND THE COLD

The bleak, dismal, frosty dusk starts
Like a cloud of snow.
A brown-feathered owl, sits on a dusty post,
Like a rag doll, that was left.
A red-breasted robin, tucks its head into its body,
Like a boy in his bed.
A swift, grey squirrel scuttles to its dray
Like a speeding bullet.
The bare trees glisten in the misty moonlight,
Like a crystal in the light.
The night moves on, all is still,
Like a stone on the floor.
A spider's web glistens in the moonlight,
Like a silk string -
A trout hides in its winter home,
Like a conker in its conker shell.
A duck flying south,
Like a scared mouse.
'Tis though winter
Has lost power.

*William Ruff (10)*
*Hutton Rudby Primary School*

## THE AWAKENING OF THE MORN

The fragile grass is scattered with frost,
Glistening like silver diamonds in the tranquil sun.
Little mice scurry along rocks,
Finding a place to hide, somewhere to go.
The morning sun beams,
It yawns, stretching its wide mouth,
Hiding the faint blackness of the sky.

Hidden in a bed of leaves chirps a red-breasted robin,
Who is the proud ruler of the gnarled tree.
Small cars cough as they struggle to wake up
So early in the morning.
Sequin-like stars disappear,
Seeming to cascade down a sunlit waterfall.

The sky glows a warm pink and peach colour.
The sound of cars starts to get louder,
Getting up and groaning.
Now the faint blackness of the sky has disappeared,
Cobwebs are broken and the sound of people talking
Is in the distance.
The silhouette of trees is there no longer,
As the majestic sun rises up into the morning's horizon.

*Hannah Whittingham (11)*
*Hutton Rudby Primary School*


## THE AWAKENING OF THE MORN

The dark sky starts to fade away
Bright, tranquil stars in the sky close their eyes and disappear.
A bird slowly awakens from a crooked tree and sings the
Peaceful song of the morning.
A rusty car grumbles angrily as it gets up from its sleep.
One by one street lamps melt away into nothing.

Cobwebs glisten as they hang from bare bushes.
The majestic sun rises up casting a dark silhouette of the tall buildings.
The very first alarm clock rings, echoing through an empty house.
Bent over, deformed trees mysteriously whisper to each other.
The sun lets go of its warmth as colours cascade over the sky.
The day has just begun.

*Grace Seller (11)*
*Hutton Rudby Primary School*

## THE WARM AND THE COLD

The bleak, desolate night captures day,
Leaving revenge to find his own way.
Gleaming stars appear in the sky,
Their twinkling glow shining up high.

A lazy badger in its cosy bedding
Like confetti stored in a box on a wedding.
Lakes tucked up under a white sheet of snow,
Just listening to the frosted wind blow.

An energetic hare bounds, silhouetting against the moon,
Like water running off each side of a spoon.
A startled raven flies into the night
Like a glinting star appearing into sight.

Black, scuttling woodlouse sleeps under rocks
Silently creeping like a sly, ginger fox.
Slowly crystal snowflakes pirouette through the air
Quickly freezing everywhere.

Then the sun peeps over a hill, casting her shadow over the land.

*Melissa Darwent (10)*
*Hutton Rudby Primary School*

## THE LAST AUTUMN DAYS

The soft, silky, spider webs gracefully swaying,
a cold corner.
The gentle raindrops gather in a small space.
The jewelled visible shiny web faded.

The leaves, dancing in a circle till they hit the
hard ground, landing in abundance.
The mournful trees light up with colours,
As they curl up, the texture disappears, leaving leaves behind.

The birds migrating south,
The birds left behind swim in pools of leaves.
Squirrels gather shiny nuts for the winter.
Animals hibernate in a bed of evergreen plants.
Golden patchwork fields are there again.

The sun is going down,
People see the first snowflakes landing softly.
The moon is lit p with joy,
Destiny's child has shut the door to autumn.

*Emma Charlton (10)*
*Hutton Rudby Primary School*


## THE MORNING SONG

The dark, lonely night sky retreats
And the majestic sunset peers over the hill,
Claiming his rightful throne in the sky.
The swift blackbird soars across the sky,
Like a floating hang-glider.

The peaceful, fluffy squirrel awakens from his sleep
And searches for crunchy nuts.
The gnarled, twisted tree whispers in the wind
And talks to the serene butterflies that dance in the air.

The calm, colourful flowers sway in the wind,
Like they are waving to a long-lost friend.
The proud bees zip around like they are insane.
All lights go out as the sun casts his fishing net of light
Over the land.

*Sam Malone (10)*
*Hutton Rudby Primary School*


## ON A MOONLIT NIGHT

In the distance the lights of the heavens switch on,
The constellation of Orion stands out like a
purple feather on a dove;
The mysterious figure walked down the
glimmering water's edge.
The mystical sky and her moon,
shoot silvery beams at the Earth,
Rustling leaves fall, pirouetting down into the
pale shadows of people coming out of the pub.
Slumbering towns sleep peacefully in the infinite
beauty of the Earth's clutches.
Trees whisper to each other, dancing on the
fathomless distances of dazzling moonlight.
A smoky smell comes from the houses
which had just put out their fires.
A translucent light shimmers on the path,
Little mice scuttle, trying not to be caught by the
great barn owl, flying gently along behind them
waiting to attack.
The night dies away and the light of the heavens
goes out.
Morning has arrived.

*Charlotte Bennington (10)*
*Hutton Rudby Primary School*

## UP INTO THE ATTIC

I open the big oak door with a rusty key
And begin to climb the foot-worn staircase.
I see old photographs in flaky, gilt frames
Lining the walls of the dark passage.
Nobody is smiling.
I reach the top of the stairs
And find another big door.
I push it open
And as my eyes get used to the gloom
I see a room full of treasure
Waiting to be found.
As I go into the musty attic and switch on the dusty light
A startled spider scuttles into a crack
As the floor opens its mouth to let it in.
I move forward into the attic
And see a beautiful doll,
Its china face smiles back at me.
I open a dusty chest, it is filled with old clothes.
I open lots more chests and look at the contents,
Things that haven't been touched for years,
Then I go down the ladder and close the door.
The attic will wait generations to be looked at again.

*Kate Simpson (10)*
*Hutton Rudby Primary School*


## SMALL DAWN SONG

This is just to say thank you to the grandfather clock
Like an army sentry marching slowly.

The low star glinting in the bleak, black sky,
Slowly it disappears.

To the lorry with glinting, gleaming eyes
Flicking on and off in the cold dark.

The awakening sun is pushing the bleak, black sky away
And majestic colours unleash slowly.

This is just to say thank you.

*Martin Lane (11)*
*Hutton Rudby Primary School*

## ODE TO AUTUMN

The sun rises giving the Earth a silhouetted blanket
of imaginative colours,
The lazy hedgehog scutters around in the mournful mist,
They are trying to find a soft-bedded earth to hibernate in
through winter and wake up in the silent spring.
As apples ripen, trees bend, trying hard to push
the lovely, juicy, red apples off.
They sink down through the grey mist, dripping
on to the muddy ground.
The leaves pirouetting down from high branches
The soft, furry badgers settle down to sleep
through the cold days of winter.
The farmers all work hard in the patchwork fields
getting ready the crops for harvest.
Birds migrate to warmer places and come back in summer.
As winter grows, days get colder and the last lonely leaf
falls off the trees.
Snowflakes fall from the sky, covering the Earth
with winter's blanket.
It covers every thing about autumn.
All the animals will be curled up in a deep sleep.

*Stephanie Williams (10)*
*Hutton Rudby Primary School*

## AWAKENING OF THE MORNING

The sun rises

As the awaking blackbird stands proudly
On the gnarled tree,
As the fading stars twinkle and vanish.

The sun rises

As the grumbling dustbin lorry sighs
And moves on.
The car's eyes shut as it lies peacefully
On the rough drive
And the disappearing lamps go off
One by one.

The sun rises

As the busy spider spins a new web.
The lively blackbird dives down
And catches a wiggling worm.

The sun rises

And the awaking of the morning goes on.

*Becky Innes (11)*
*Hutton Rudby Primary School*


## ON A MOONLIT NIGHT

The crescent moon emerges casting its cape over the world.
The majestic stars wink at me as I stride by.
A tranquil forest reaches out as if it was trying to pull me in.
The old, gnarled trees glare at me, sending a chill down my spine.
Prickly hedgehogs scurrying about searching for food.
I see a glow in the distance;
I realise that the sun is returning to its throne.

I sit on a hill, watching the majestic sun
Fighting for the right to be in the sky.
As I sit watching, a tear falls from my cheek,
But I realise it will be back.
The sun stands proud in the sky, beaming down at the Earth.
I will never forget the secrets that the night has shared with me.

*Thomas Ruff (10)*
*Hutton Rudby Primary School*


## ON A MOONLIT NIGHT

As I finish my hard paper round, I see the moonlit sky,
full of stars.
The claws of darkness have driven the sun out of its throne
and it is proclaimed king of the skies.
The first evening star is the biggest and brightest,
The full moon is in joy as he rises to the sky once again.
The bright headlights of cars switched on as drivers see
the mystical, black sky.
The forest is full of crooked figures and scares people away
from its boundaries.
The bright eyes of an owl seeks its prey as it hunts,
unnoticed by anyone.
The constellations are shining brighter than ever before,
As they fly into the night sky.
The bright green eyes of a cat, stalking silently after its
noisy prey.
The barking of a dog, like the shouting of a parent.
The wind blowing the trees, like an army of men pushing
them down.
The moon gently fades away and day has won once again.

*James Walton (11)*
*Hutton Rudby Primary School*

## A Silent Night

It was a cold, frosty night
I sat on my bed
The frost sparkled
It was all white
I pulled back my curtains to see a child . . .
She was pale,
Her clothes shining,
Her white hair was glittering,
Almost like a star.
I watched as she turned around,
I watched
Fascinated to see her float across the garden,
She looked like an angel,
She flew in the distance.
'Please don't go,' I said,
As she turned around and smiled
And pointed at the moon
I looked up but when I looked down she had gone,
I closed my curtains and lay down.
I closed my eyes and fell into a deep sleep.
Every night I see her sparkling in the moonlight,
Her hair,
Her clothes
And the frost.

*Ashlee Sharp (11)*
*Kirkby Fleetham CE School*

## THE CREATURE

The creature creeps,
Eyes shining, teeth glimmering.
Silently he prowls the cave,
Tail swishing, claws scratching.
Hunting for his prey,
Wings folded, spikes set back.
What's that? His prey!
It's moving in the water.
Silently he creeps nearer,
Suddenly he pounces! Prey turns round,
Seconds too late,
Creature grabs! Tears! Rips!
Prey is down, creature eats.
Men are coming,
Voices ring in the cave, creature tries to escape.
Men are coming,
Rifle is raised,
*Bang!*
Creature falls!
Men approach, spikes unfold,
Men's cries echo round the cave.
Spikes fire but creature knows he is done.
Creature and men alike, lie in the cave.

***Duncan Mason (11)***
***Kirkby Fleetham CE School***

## THE DARK, DARK PLACE

In a dark, dark field,
Is a dark, dark forest,
In the dark, dark forest,
Is a dark, dark lake,
At the end of the dark, dark lake,
Is a dark, dark mansion,
In the dark, dark mansion,
Is a dark, dark corridor,
At the end of the dark, dark corridor,
Is a dark, dark cupboard,
In the dark, dark cupboard,
Is a dark, dark box,
In the dark, dark box,
There's a dark, dark *spider!*

***Joshua Atkinson (10)***
***Kirkby Fleetham CE School***


## WITCH'S SPELL

Take lizards' feet and snakes' slime,
Piglets' hooves and a drop of wine.
Add herb and spice and all things nice,
A bit of herb and rice.
Cows' horns and some ear wax,
Finch's tongue and a few facts,
A dab of glitter and a cat's scratch
And a bit of bitter and a patch.

Say the magic words
And there you have:
An enemy turned into a
*Frog!*

***Katy Gill (10)***
***Kirkby Fleetham CE School***

## THE BATTLE OF THE KNIGHT

The sword slashes against his skin
Blood trickles down his face
And his eyes sparkle in the sun.
As he lies there he thinks of his love,
The one that died for him.
As the man draws closer, closer, closer
He sees a man in the distance
Riding for the killer
And in the light he sees the killer
Fall to the ground,
Blood surrounds the grass
In the distance he sees the knight, riding, riding,
Riding into the sun.

*Sam Toothill (11)*
*Kirkby Fleetham CE School*


## THE WINDY DAY

Yesterday the wind was blowing,
The trees were falling,
A gust of wind blew the leaves,
Roof tiles shook the house,
The wind was wild that day.

Lorries overturning on the motorway,
Haystacks collapsing,
Hair going wild,
Umbrellas turning inside out,

The wind was wild that day.

*Rachel Tiplady (10)*
*Kirkby Fleetham CE School*

## THE WITCH'S CUPBOARD

Open the door
Boxes, bottles and jars fill the shelves
With magic
Tongue of bat, leg of toad,
Bottles, potions make a brew.
Dolphin's tooth and eel's slime
Cats' eyes stored in a jar
Wand and broomstick, cauldron too,
Powders, liquids, pills and more.
A skeleton hangs on the door,
Spiders' webs cover the hinges,
Spell books covered in dust
Feathers and sticks
The witch lights a fire and greases her cauldron!
*Beware the witch's cupboard.*

**Harriet Henderson (9)**
**Kirkby Fleetham CE School**


## THE EYES

The eyes gleaming
In the moonlit stars,
Sparkling like diamonds,
The colours like a rainbow.

They're moving closer and closer
I shiver! I can't move,
I'm stuck to the ground.
It stops! Is it looking at me?
No it's looking at its dinner.

It jumps, I jump,
I hear a scream,
Not any scream; a cry
The eyes jump
Into the light.

*What is it?*

***Lois Jermyn  (10)***
***Kirkby Fleetham CE School***

# GUESS WHO?

She is a windy gale, a funny clown
She is tight, smart clothes
A clock ringing always at dawn
She is a grown-up four
A green grass countryside
She is a soft, sweet voice
A computer working hard all the time
She is a lovely flower sprouting in spring
A bright, sunny colour
She is a packet of crisps
A sweet candy
She is a newborn puppy
A galloping horse
She is a soft, silk settee
A fine posh room
She is posh, shiny shoes.

***David Leighton  (8)***
***Langcliffe Primary School***

## MY BROTHER!

He's a blood-red apple rolling down a hill
He's a tornado and punk rocker clothes
A monster truck lorry at 90mph
A bad mood storming
And a power plant ready to explode
He's a rose bush with spiky thorns
A kitchen with a million pounds of food
*A big, mean teatime machine*
He's a devil's soft toy
A roaring lion hunting
An angry voice echoing
He's America with power
He's a lavatory!

***Thomas Lee (9)***
***Langcliffe Primary School***


## MY BROTHER MARK

He's a bobcat
An early morning starter
He's a cheeseburger
He's a dairy farm, a cowshed
A silage pit and a straw shed
He's a wagon, a Scania parked up
He's a JCB forklift moving muck
He's a forty-five foot trailer
Ready with a unit.

***Daniel Newhouse (9)***
***Langcliffe Primary School***

## MY LITTLE SISTER

Her colour is blue
She's a calm voice
And a busy vacuum cleaner
Or a little cleaning-up vehicle
Wanting to tidy up
She's a sunflower
And a calm sun in the sky
She's a quiet mouse and very neat
Up early in the morning
She's the black mane of a horse
She's black and white for school
She's a Barbie
And a tall building standing up high.

*Charlotte Jeffrey (7)*
*Langcliffe Primary School*


## WHICH BOY?

He's red and orange spots
And he's sunny when girls go by
With a voice as loud as a horn
He's a wagon
He's a football bouncing up and down
A skyscraper as tall as two trees
A phone line to girls
A Cheshire cat
He's a pet bunny, nibbling cabbage
A Goofy cartoon
He's a chunky KitKat.

*Imogen Pilling (9)*
*Langcliffe Primary School*

## THE BOY!

He's a bungalow
He's a baby reptile
He's the sun with glasses on
Or a rabbit with long ears
A dandelion that's been picked
He's sporty clothes with spots
And he's honey-brown
He's a squeaky mouse
He's a Fudge bar, on the shelf.

*Alexandra Jeffrey (10)*
*Langcliffe Primary School*


## THREE FRIENDS

There is a gang of three,
Stuart, Chris and me.
We play out in the park,
Sometimes when it's dark.
Our mothers always shout,
Oh, I wish we could stay out.

We shelter from the rain
That rushes down the drain,
We kick our ball about.
Oh, I wish we could stay out.

We like to build our den,
But only now and then.
Look, the sun's come out,
Hooray, we can stay out.

*Hayden Goodwin (9)*
*Le Cateau Community School*

## BERKIM

There was once a Berkim bird,
That lived in a Tumtum tree.

When the sea was still,
You could hear the Berkim's pleasant chirping,
It chirped all day, it chirped all night.

Berkim could not fly, so it hopped instead.
If Berkim fell, then it would roll
Until it hit a tree.

Berkim was camouflaged,
It hid in the bushes all day long,
But at night, it played with its friend,
The Jubjub bird.

*Kimberley Mossman (11)*
*Le Cateau Community School*


## FLIBBER-FLAB

The Flibber-Flab did scrill and scroll
Upon the shining moon,
Calling for old Bridal-Bral,
His mad old friend, the loon.

He scrambled over lava lumps,
All around that sloughy bog.
He could not see old Bridal-Bral,
For the dense and smoggly fog.

The Flibber-Flab did scrowl and prowl,
So desperate for old Bridal-Bral.
He found him in the Whatsthat Tree,
Bridal-Bral said, 'Were you looking for me?'

*Rebecca Hall (11)*
*Le Cateau Community School*

## GONE AGAIN

I joined the army,
A gypsy type of life,
Four lovely children,
A martyr for a wife.

The job is a nuisance,
A bit of a pain,
Kids get fed up,
I'm going away again.

Silence is golden,
So say we all,
Gets a bit annoying,
The kids stuck to the wall.

The phone's a lifeline,
Bills are quite high,
Time I must be going
To fly in the sky.

R 'n' R has ended,
I have to be gone.
The kids are grounded,
The wife has to stay strong.

*Chantelle Lyal (9)*
*Le Cateau Community School*


## SCHOOL YARD

Children playing one, two, three,
Laughing, shouting, happy as can be.
Boys playing football in the yard,
Girls are huddled in a squad.

Teacher comes and blows the whistle,
All the children turn and listen.
One by one the classes go,
'Hurry up and don't be slow.'

*Shannon-Lea Alder (10)*
*Le Cateau Community School*

## CLIMBING MOUNT EVEREST

Determined to climb in my mind,
While getting higher, my mind was on fire,
Gasping for air,
Waiting to be first up there.
Getting higher, I was freezing,
I finally reached the summit.

Determined to climb in our minds,
While getting higher, our minds were on fire,
Gasping for air, trying to get up there,
Waiting to be first to the summit.
As we were getting higher, we were freezing,
Wondering, just wondering if we were going to survive.
At last, we reached the summit.

Going back down, slipping and sliding,
Getting nearer and nearer to the foot.
We were getting warmer and warmer while going down.
We finally reached the foot
Where the lovely green land is.
We were glad to be back down.

*Apryl Kennedy (10)*
*Le Cateau Community School*

## THE CLIMB TO EVEREST!

The three men were quivering from head to toe,
Wondering what it would feel like
To be at the top of the summit.
One by one, they climbed rock by rock,
Whimpering they were, frigid and numb
As they staggered and stumbled, rock by rock,
Gasping for oxygen.
Halfway up they felt like giving up,
But they knew that they had climbed so far.
But they carried on climbing, rock by rock,
Nearly frozen from head to toe.
They carried on whimpering,
While their fingers went blue.
Exhausted they were, not confident anymore,
Two miles to climb, they couldn't believe it.
'Yes, yes!' they shouted.
They were finally at the summit.

*Charlotte Mott (10)*
*Le Cateau Community School*


## THE STRUGGLE OF EVEREST

The worried mind determined to get safely up,
Starting to struggle up the crystal icicles,
Body temperature lowering,
Gasping for a drink.
My hands are going blue,
Body temperature below 10°C,
Staggering miles to go to the summit.

At the middle, stopped for a bite to eat,
Carry on going,
Hard to breathe,
Keep on going, starting to freeze.
Near to the top,
One more step,
I've achieved my goal.

*Marc Bullimore (10)*
*Le Cateau Community School*

## A JOURNEY TO THE TOP OF A MOUNTAIN

When I stood at the foot of Mount Everest,
I was determined I could do it.
I kept on climbing until my fingers were blue.
I stumbled a few times,
I felt tired and weary,
Tired and dreamy,
Ten miles to go.
Clinging to rocks, I pushed myself
Until I finally reached the top of the mountain.

It was just like my dream,
It was a beautiful landscape.
Gasping for breath,
Freezing cold,
I sat down on the summit.
I felt proud of myself.

*Abigail Mortimer (9)*
*Le Cateau Community School*

## COLOURS

There are lots of different colours in the rainbow,
There are lots of different colours in the sea,
There are lots of different colours in the whole wide world,
Including you and me.

Red like the blood that flows through your veins,
Yellow the sun that gives us all life,
Green the trees that clean the air,
Blue the sky and the birds that are there.

All these different colours make up our world,
Out of all these different colours, my favourite is *blue*.

*Tayler Froehling (10)*
*Le Cateau Community School*


## THE SUN AND THE MOON

The sun shines like an orange in the sky,
The moon shines bright, but only at night.
The sun came out to play one day
And frightened poor little moon away.
The glowing light danced in the sky,
Gliding slowly, right up high.

The moon was peering, being shy,
Watching the sun up in the sky.
Moon moved slowly nearer to the sun,
Who was so tired and then was gone.

*Christopher Stewart (9)*
*Le Cateau Community School*

## EVEREST

H ilary and Tenzing were at the foot of Everest
I n determined minds and confident souls.
M onstrous slopes as they start to climb
A nd their fingers were turning blue.
L azy legs need a rest only after just stopping,
A mazing views from all around fill their minds with joy,
Y et so far to go, you can see the foot one mile below.
A strange thing happens, Tenzing begins to choke,
S o Tenzing bashing ice in his air tank was able to breathe once again.

I n the snow does Hilary fall with a weary body,
N othing can stop them now.

T he exhausted couple pitch tent for the night
I n the freezing, icy snow.
B elow freezing was the temperature.
E ven though the wind was creeping,
T here was nothing to stop determined minds and confident souls.

*Zack Eddie (10)*
*Le Cateau Community School*

## A PANDA

A black and white panda,
Strolling through the forests of China.
A panda, a panda, a panda,
Sitting in the shade under big, green leaves,
Chewing on bamboo.
A panda, a panda, a panda,
Cuddly and furry,
Snuggling up in bed.
A panda, a panda, a panda.

*Leanne Smith (9)*
*Longman's Hill CP School*

## ON THE PING PANG PONG

On the Ping Pang Pong
Where everything goes wrong
And the dudes all say, 'What's up?'
There's a Pong Pang Ping
Where the monkeys sing
And the jellies go wibble, wobble, woo.
On the Pong Ping Pang
All the pigs talk slang
And you can't get on down when they do,
So it's Ping Pang Pong,
Donkey King Kong,
Pong Pang Ping,
Aaron can't sing.
Pong Ping Pang,
What's up man?
What a cool place to belong,
Is the Ping Pang Ping Pang Pong.

*Adam Smith (9)*
*Longman's Hill CP School*

## A BLAZE

A blaze is always smoking,
Scorched fur sticks up in fright,
Burnt whiskers like fuse wire,
*Pop!* He's set alight.

The sparks are rising,
Crackle, crackle!
His ears stick up like spikes,
Sparkle, sparkle!

*Sophie-Jade Marshall (10)*
*Longman's Hill CP School*

## DOLPHIN BLUE

Under the ocean,
Swimming with motion,
You'll find some creatures
With wonderful features.

They're grey and smooth,
Their delicate move,
Their smiling face!
What a disgrace?

Alert they keep,
Avoiding to seek
The dreaded net,
The line to death.

*Amelia Vickers (11)*
*Longman's Hill CP School*


## DEAR MUM

Dear Mum,

While you were out,
The cat pooed on the mobile,
Maybe it saw something terrible.

The dog jumped into the pool
Out of the very top window,
It went three metres deep!
The dogs are going like crazy.

Everywhere's haunted!

Love, Sam.

*Sam Bruce (9)*
*Longman's Hill CP School*

## OH THANK YOU, HOW KIND OF YOU

Oh thank you, how kind of you,
Just what I needed.
It's a small blue one with buttons.
How you have succeeded
In making my day.
I'm so overwhelmed, what more can I say?
You couldn't have got better,
Obviously not cheap,
It's rather annoying, those horrible beeps.
It can be quite handy,
It fits in its case,
Don't let it get scratched
And it can stand on its base.
I can ring my friends,
I can ring round the bend.
The screen is perfect,
It's the right size for me,
I can take it where I like,
I can take it to the sea.
I got a brand new cover
And a screensaver I'll keep,
It's a beautiful gift
And its finish exquisite,
Though I have been thinking,
It's nice, but what is it?

*Jamie Hambrecht (9)*
*Longman's Hill CP School*

## NEVER-ENDING CHASE

I'm running, so catch me.
Come on, catch me and push me into a tree!
You will never, ever track me down,
I will be here, there and everywhere.

When you have found your prize,
You will be ecstatic in glory,
But something strange will appear, then disappear.
Goodbye my friend, this is the end.

*Joshua Gibbon (11)*
*Longman's Hill CP School*


## SCHOOL

Bell ringer,
Door swinger,
Pen chewer,
Homework doer.
Loud talker,
Slow walker,
Sum solver,
Spell checker,
Computer huddler,
Science lover.
Big laugher,
Great clapper,
English nerd,
History first.
Coat swinger,
Soppy kisser,
Big farter,
Nose picker,
Nail chewer,
Home runner.
School rules - not!

*Natalie Hambrecht (11)*
*Longman's Hill CP School*

## IT'S A BULL'S LIFE

I'm getting angry,
People are whipping me for no reason.
What should I do?
Shall I fight back,
Or walk away?
He's getting closer.
I turned and ran,
Then he ran after me.
I turned back and struck back at him.
My horns caught his red cloak,
He was getting angry.
One whip and I was in so much pain
I could barely walk.
I got up onto two feet,
He whipped me again and I fell back down.
I daren't get up,
I'm slowly dying.
I feel weak . . .

*Nathan Parker (11)*
*Longman's Hill CP School*


## MAGIC UNDER THE SEA

The waves crash on the rocks,
War is on the land,
Under the sea it is quiet,
Where every sea animal gets on.
I wish I could be there
Instead of on this land of death.
Under the sea, it's like magic
And every little thing's unique.

On land, we take it for granted
And no magic can be set free,
So this land will always be
The land of death.
But the magic of the sea won't stay magic
If we keep polluting it.
It will just be like the land,
The land of death.

*Holly Ness (11)*
*Longman's Hill CP School*

## IT'S NICE, BUT WHAT IS IT?

Oh thank you! How kind of you!
Just what I needed!
It's a brown thing,
How you have succeeded
In making my Christmas.
I'm so overwhelmed,
What more can I say?

It's made out of wood,
It's brown,
It goes on water,
You can ride on it,
You can travel.
It's beautiful
And its finish exquisite,
Though I have been thinking,
It's nice, but what is it?

*Mathew Weston (9)*
*Longman's Hill CP School*

## HORSE LOVER

Horse lover,
Trotting off,
Lovely colour,
Lovely nuzzler.

Horse lover,
Cantering off,
Swishing his tail
In the blue.

Horse lover
Galloping off,
Into the water,
Like the crashing waves.

*Amy Williams (10)*
*Longman's Hill CP School*


## PRAISE SONG OF THE WIND

Hinges on doors, not lightly on,
I will crash. I, the wind,
I will roar, I will whistle.

Bikes which are left outside
I will smash. I, the wind,
I will roar, I will whistle.

People who are walking
I will kill. I, the wind,
I will roar, I will whistle.

*Lee Moore (10)*
*Longman's Hill CP School*

## THE SEED

The seed that lies upon the ground
Does shimmer in the heat.
It makes not a sound.
Not much bigger than the tip of my feet.

The roots grip below the earth,
No one can see beneath the yard.
Breaking up out of the turf,
Rising up to the sun's guard.

See the stem grow high
Above the soil, so black and dry.
The motion of the stem waves so fine.

The petals come out so fine.
The wind makes a normal howl,
The colours sway and shine
Under the clouds' towel.

Seeds do drop quickly.
The bee lands so peacefully above the petal.
On the bee, the seeds stick,
On the ground they settle.

The seed that lies upon the ground
Does shimmer in the heat.
It makes not a sound.
Not much bigger than the tip of my feet.

*Lauren Littlewood (11)*
*Longman's Hill CP School*

## DEAR MUM

Dear Mum,

While you were out,
Somehow the washing machine
Has flooded the house
And somehow, your new dress
Went down the toilet.

I don't know how your best pictures got smashed
And the eggs got broken, or how the computer got broken,
And I don't know how Dads mobile phone got broken.

I don't know how your favourite vase got smashed,
And how the computer blew up
And how the window got broken.
I was being good, honest,
Knowing you're going to have a fit,
I've gone to Gran's for a bit.

Love, Jake.

*Jake Marshall (9)*
*Longman's Hill CP School*


## DEEP DOWN IN THE BIG, BLUE SEA

Deep down in the big, blue sea,
Amazing things, what can you see?
Abandoned ships lying on the floor,
The deeper you go, you see more and more.

There lies the chest under the sand
On the floor, in a faraway land.
Pirates' treasure then, in a big ship,
The waves are crashing, the treasure has tipped.

Down I go, into the deep,
I looked around, there was not a peep.
There's the treasure, I'm going to be rich,
Is there a lock, or is there a switch?

I slowly open up the chest,
I'm going to be famous and the best.
No one could find it years ago,
Back to the submarine I go.

*Courtney Graves (10)*
*Longman's Hill CP School*

## DEAR MUM

Dear Mum,

While you were out,
Somehow your favourite ornament got smashed.
I don't know how the cat got outside,
Somehow a burglar got in and I got bashed.

Somehow, the cat had an accident on your bed.
When I went down, the other cat was dead.
The dog must have drawn on the curtains with a pencil lead.

I don't know how your TV blew up,
And I don't know why the dog started acting like a pup.
I don't know how the rabbit found a carrot
And how the dog nearly ate the parrot.
I was being good, honest.
Knowing you're going to have a fit,
I've gone round to Nan's for a bit.

Love, Kirsten.

*Kirsten MacGregor (9)*
*Longman's Hill CP School*

## GOOD MORNING AND WELCOME TO THE TEACHER WEATHER FORECAST!

Mrs Parker,
Will cause severe ink floods around the school
Due to pen leakages.
Mr Lewis
Will be mild, but around mid-afternoon,
There will be shooting soccer plunging to the ground.
Mr Peirs,
At the start of the day, Mr Peirs will be thundering down a few kids
But will return to his normal sunny self.
Mrs Robson
Is already gusting down with her dinner list and
Should reach gale force 7 when she hits her office.
Mrs Carpenter,
Some paint is expected around Mrs Carpenter,
She has not quite got enough of her brushing gales.
As for the rest of you, it will be much as usual,
A mixture of thunderstorms and patches of sunshine
                                        in a few classrooms.
Have an eventful day!

*Emma Cook (10)*
*Longman's Hill CP School*

## MY GREAT WALK

Walking through the city,
A big city it is,
I see loads of things
And here are a few.

Buildings as tall as beanstalks
Stretching up to the sky,
Lights as bright as moonlight,
Glistening with stars,

Roads as busy as bees with their honey,
Flying all about,
Cars as fast as shooting stars,
Shooting round and round.

Now there are a few of my descriptions,
But now I have walked through the city
And have finished my great walk.

*Luke Swithenbank (10)*
*Longman's Hill CP School*

## A LIFE

You were born in January with the year as white
As the paper you're writing on at the dead of night.
February, you were eating and sleeping mashed potato,
March, you were walking and talking and you've never stopped since,
April, you went to school for your first week and asked to go
　　　　　　　　　　　　　　　for the weekend,
May, you got lost on your first day of high school and forgot
　　　　　　　　　　　　　　　your dinner money,
June, you were caught smoking and always on the mobile,
And got caught snogging your girlfriend,
July, got a job at a Chinese takeaway in the kitchens,
August, got married to a solicitor and had the do in court,
September, the kids were driving you up the wall,
The woman tells you what to do.
October, the kids are grown-ups and giving you some stress,
November you're a fogie and telling everyone the truth,
December, you go to sleep as the sun goes down and the moon
　　　　　　　　　　　　　　　comes up.
You lie there with your eyes shut.

*Luke Scott (9)*
*Longman's Hill CP School*

# A LIFE

You were born in January, with the year as white
As the paper you're writing on, at dead of night.
In February, you got some hair and started to crawl,
In March you started to walk and talk,
Then your mum told you to shut up.
In April, you went to school and tripped over the teacher's foot,
In May you went to high school and got detention for homework,
In June you got a boyfriend and got drunk in the toilets,
In July you got a job running a pizza shop,
In August, you got kids and lost your voice, shouting,
In September, you got soppy and went to the pub,
In October you got older and moved to a big house,
In November, you were 94, had a party and grew grey hair,
In December, you were asleep in the chair and never woke up again.

*Michelle Scott (10)*
*Longman's Hill CP School*


# DEAR MUM

Dear Mum,

While you were out,
Somehow the dog wanted to take a bath
And now all your best towels are dirty.
I don't know how your best dress has gone bright yellow,
I don't know why the phone is in the sink,
I don't know how tomato sauce is all over the house,
I don't know how the juggling balls have gone through the windows,
I don't know how the stick insects are laying in your bed.
I was being good, honest.
Knowing you're going to have a fit,
I've gone to Gran's for a bit.

*Denika Yorke (10)*
*Longman's Hill CP School*

## DEAR MUM

Dear Mum,

While you were out,
Somehow the fish tank smashed
And drenched the floor.

The cat somehow got on your bed and wet it,
Plus the TV's got my shoe in.
I don't know how the rabbit got under the shed.

I don't know how your dress got into the toilet,
I don't know how the dog got so far,
I was being good, honest.
Knowing you're going to have a fit,
I've gone to Gran's for a bit.

Love, Gordon.

*Gordon Wilkinson (9)*
*Longman's Hill CP School*


## MOON MOLES

They plough through the brown moody mud.
They lift the moon's skin like a tawny-green bramble bush
Standing all alone in the middle of a deserted, cold, dark place.
A rich emerald on the ground, a twitch.
They plunge deep,
Their eyes never open, but they still glare and stare.
Their skin smoothes the moon's surface,
Their feet and hands are the rocky boulders of the night.
If you get up there, you will see the magical, surprising,
Rarest creatures burning bright, all through the night.

*Fay Horn (11)*
*Longman's Hill CP School*

## IT'S NICE, BUT WHAT IS IT?

Oh, thank you! How kind of you!
Just what I needed!
It's small.
How you have succeeded
In making my Christmas,
In making my day.
What more can I say?
It's not big, the vehicle,
You can play with it,
You can get all kinds of bases and aircraft carriers,
The vehicles have wheels.
It's a beautiful gift
And its finish exquisite,
Though I have been thinking,
It's nice, but what is it?

***Geraint Thomas  (9)***
***Longman's Hill CP School***

## SPRING

Spring is the most beautiful time of year,
Swaying daffodils in the breeze,
Flowers blooming,
Baby lambs in the fields,
The sun shining brightly,
Everyone loves spring.

The time of year the world becomes beautiful,
Blossom starts to come out on trees,
Lovely smelling flowers,
The smell of the daffodils,
Entrance my heart.

***Katherine Wright  (9)***
***Longman's Hill CP School***

## HIDDEN TREASURES

Long, long ago, on a deserted sea,
There was a deserted lighthouse,
And in that deserted lighthouse
There was a deserted room,
And . . . oh no!
There was a code on the door,
But right in the middle of the floor
Was the . . . answer!
Open the door, creak, creak,
I can hear a noise, squeak, squeak,
But never mind all that,
Look, here it is!
Diamonds, silver, rubies and gold,
All my secret treasures are here!

*Anna Stockil (9)*
*Markington CE Primary School*


## HIDDEN TREASURE

Hidden treasure, where could it be?
I'll dig in the garden and see.
Dig, dig, quick, quick, before anyone sees me.
It's hot out here, I need a rest.
Wait a minute, wait a minute,
What's this? A silver box.
Let's open it and see.
Oh no! It needs a key.
There it is, let's open it then.
Wow!
It is a bright, red . . . diamond!

*Christie Johnson (8)*
*Markington CE Primary School*

## HIDDEN TREASURES

One day I went to the seaside,
I was strolling along the shore.
To my amazement, I saw a cave
In the side of the rocky cliff.
I wandered over to the dark, gloomy cave,
Cautiously crept in.
At the back of the cave I looked.
A rotted, musty old chest,
Lodged firmly in the back of the wall.
I remembered a key my great grandad had given to me
And I tried it in the lock.
It opened the chest.
It was full of beautiful gems.
I pushed the riches aside
To find my great grandad's most treasured possession,
It was a little, damp teddy bear.
Out loud I exclaimed, 'Thank you!'

*Daniel Flanagan (11)*
*Markington CE Primary School*


## HIDDEN TREASURES

Treasures, treasures underground,
Dig, dig, dig.
Always have to dig!
Always have to dig!
Dig, dig, dig,
Don't know why?
Always have to dig,
Gold, diamonds, rubies and coins.
Dig, dig, dig.

*Anya Johnson (8)*
*Markington CE Primary School*

## HIDDEN TREASURES

Far away in
Eastern lands
Many secrets lie.

Above the hills,
Beyond the sun,
Someone hears a cry.

Along a quiet and dusty road
A little old rag lies,
Strewn across the muddy ground.

I think I see it,
Then I don't,
My mind is in a whirl.

Then I stop and think
For a little while.
What a lovely possession,
Not gold, not diamonds,
But a little old rag, worn and torn.
What a great hidden treasure.

*Daniel Wilberforce (11)*
*Markington CE Primary School*


## HIDDEN TREASURE

My treasure is not like any other.
It is not coins or rubies.
It doesn't cost anything at all,
It is at home and it is
The best of them all.
My treasure is my mum!

*Callum Otley (10)*
*Markington CE Primary School*

## HIDDEN TREASURE

Deep down in my brother
Is a hidden treasure.
Even though he is annoying,
He can be a pleasure.

It's all very nice -
Candy and cakes,
But what I like best
Are the ones he makes.

I'm sure when he dies
He'll go up to Heaven,
But I guess I shouldn't think that,
Because he's only seven.

So I hope you can tell
And easily see
That me and my brother
Live in perfect harmony.

*Katie Bates (10)*
*Markington CE Primary School*


## HIDDEN TREASURES

I went by myself into a deep, dark garage,
That had cobwebs on an old car,
And in the darkest corner of the room,
I saw a bright, golden jar.

I went striding across over a concrete floor,
Then I saw a big, open chest.
It looked so old and bare,
Then I saw the very best.

I was looking straight at a pot of gold,
Overflowing with wealth.
I got as much as I could
And carried it out all by myself.

*Andrew Schofield (11)*
*Markington CE Primary School*

## HIDDEN TREASURES

Coming and going,
I'm never at home,
Today I'm looking for treasure.
On a clear, hot, sunny day,
The sea is calm and turquoise blue
And the treasure is at the bottom.
Diving down, the fish scatter,
Right, left, forward, backwards.
What was that? I think I saw the treasure.
Big, wide, brown with metal patters,
The chest, it's here.
Grab the nearest swordfish,
The chest, it's open.
Pearls, rubies red, giant diamonds, is that all?
I hoped for gold cups,
Things fit for a king.
Is this all I get?
I'm off home,
I'm fed up.
The jewels may be precious,
But I've got loads!

*Emma Foster (10)*
*Markington CE Primary School*

## DARK NIGHT

In a dark, dark wood, on a dark, dark night,
There stands a house in the moonlight.
Inside a fire is burning bright,
Who would live there, who might?
As I wandered into the house,
I spotted on the floor a little mouse.
Into the kitchen I went and heard . . .
A scream, a laugh, then a silence emerged.
Up the stairs I crept with fright,
Suddenly appeared a little light.
Arrgghh! It was a ghost.
To my amazement it began to boast!
I ran to the door, it was locked,
I was terrified and shocked.
'Come here, my pretty,' a witch said to me,
When suddenly, I was under a tree,
Then in a desert, then in the air,
Next I was me again, under the stair.
Was it a dream? I'll never know.

*Zoe Wolstenholme (10)*
*North & South Cowton Primary School*


## HIDDEN TREASURE

Dolphins splashing in the sea,
Looking around for you and me.
I have a good day with my new friend
And I hope this day will never end.

Diving down to the seabed,
I kiss the dolphin on his head.
I clambered on the dolphin's back
And there below was a treasure sack.

The dolphin guided me by the hand
And lifted the treasure up to the sand.
I had a great day with my new friend
And I'm sad that this day had to end.

*Chloe Edwards (9)*
*North & South Cowton Primary School*

## MYSTERY IN SPACE

It was a cold, wet night,
There was a shining light.
The spacemen went to see,
It looked like a magic key.
But when they got there,
They started to stare,
What was this mysterious thing?
It sounded like it started to sing,
This thing with green and yellow spots
Has pink hair full of lots of knots.
His legs shone like a gold banana,
He had blue, stripy pyjamas.
The spacemen started to wonder,
They thought they heard some thunder.
They asked if it could talk,
Instead it started to walk.
The spacemen tried to find his home,
Around the planet they did roam.
The spacemen decided to go back,
They went back to the spaceship to pack.

*Laura Turner (10)*
*North & South Cowton Primary School*

## The Dream That Came True

When I went to bed,
I had a lovely dream.
I dreamt of me and my friend,
Thinking of the time we had
When we went away.
We floated off into the sky
And down we lay on the nice relaxing clouds.
We gazed and watched the clowns,
Who were juggling with red balls.
Then we flew down to the ground.
When I woke up, I found it was a dream.
The next day it happened just as I had seen,
I could not believe it.
I found the red ball under my bed.
I thought how strange it was
For a dream to come true.

*Katie Wilson (8)*
*North & South Cowton Primary School*


## The Weather

I am a ray of sunshine, a bright light.
I am a drop of rain, a horrible sight.
I am a spark of lightning causing a fright.
I am a bang of thunder through the night.
I am a gust of wind, a cold breeze.
I am a gale, a strong wind to blow the trees.

*Richard Ozelton (8)*
*North & South Cowton Primary School*

## I WISH I COULD FLY

I wish I could fly
Up to the sky
To see Mars and the moon
And feel happy and free.
I'd like to fly
Up to the sky
To see Mars and the moon
And feel happy and free,
But I have to go home for my tea.

I wish I could swim
To the bottom
Of the deepest ocean
And find buried treasure.
I'd like to swim
To the bottom
Of the sea
And feel happy and free,
But I have to go home for my tea.

*Kate Harrison (8)*
*North & South Cowton Primary School*


## THE LIONS

The lion is the king of the jungle,
The lion takes what he wants.
All the animals run away
When they hear the lion roar.
His long mane sticks out like a bush.
When he runs, there is a big gush of wind.
Beware, the lion is the king of the jungle.

*Joshua Riley-Fox (8)*
*North & South Cowton Primary School*

## THE RACEHORSE MYSTERY

There was once a racehorse,
She was incredible round a course.
I called her Starlight,
But she went missing one cold night.

Who could have stolen her,
Was it Madam, or Sir?
Was it the postman or milkman,
Or was it that Old Dan?

She was popular with the pieman,
Could he have loaded her into his van?
The pieman thought she was the best,
Much, much better than all the rest.

She couldn't survive on milk or a pie,
Oh I don't half hope she is nearby.
I went to bed that night,
Just worrying about Starlight.

I wondered who had Starlight,
Were they going to be riding her in the light?
I suddenly heard 'clip-clop'
And someone shout, 'Stop!'

The next morning, I went out,
There stood Starlight with no doubt.
Who would do such a bad crime,
Because Starlight is mine, oh mine.

I wondered if the thief fed her apple cores,
Then I remembered, I forgot to shut the stable doors!

*Sarah Adamson (10)*
*North & South Cowton Primary School*

## WINTER WIND

The winter wind is grey,
It whooshes around all day,
It blows all day along the way.

The people come out to play,
The winter wind blows the sun away.
The children hold their hats on tight as they run and play
On a windy, winter's day.

The old man tries to cross the road,
The winter wind blows around his feet.
As the old man wobbles from side to side,
The winter wind just howls and laughs.

When it is time to go,
Winter wind runs to and fro
And the sun comes shining through,
To blow away the winter wind blues.

*Rebecca Howell (9)*
*North & South Cowton Primary School*


## STORM

Here comes a tornado
Rushing through the town,
It's knocking all the people down,
Striking telephone posts to the ground.
Here comes a hurricane
Blowing through the park,
It's making all the dogs bark,
And scaring people in the dark.

*Martin Clark (8)*
*North & South Cowton Primary School*

## THE HAUNTED HOUSE

A haunted house stood in the wood,
The moonlight shone as it should.
I came to the door
And there I saw
Blood scattered all over the floor.
I appeared in the house
To see a frightened little mouse.
I went to the kitchen, I saw a *ghost!*
It was eating beans on toast.
I wandered over to the stair, should I dare?
I don't care!
I climbed higher and higher, becoming lighter and lighter,
I came to a room, it looked like a tomb.
I began to sweat, what a bet.
'Aaargh!' I heard a scream, was it a dream?
I flew downstairs, not wanting to stay.
On the floor, a dead body lay.
I opened the door, I'm free!
I was happy to be me.
I ran as fast as I could through the wood.

*Nicola Wilson (10)*
*North & South Cowton Primary School*


## THE THING

I am the thing that lives in your car,
I have a son, he calls me Pa.
I am training him to be really mean,
So he will bite you, make you scream.
His brother is even worse,
He'll nick some money from your purse.

*Simon Nicholson (10)*
*North & South Cowton Primary School*

## GHOST GIRL AND HORSE

In the midnight hour, above the tower,
Dreams come true in the sky so blue.
A horse ran past, I'd seen him at last.
A girl ran by, singing a lullaby.
A total mystery, modern history,
Were they dead or alive?
A ghost girl and horse, heading on course,
The ghost girl whirled, the ghost horse twirled,
Jumping over stars, flying over Mars.
The girl caught the horse and led him with no force
Towards the sunbeams, just like in my dreams
Would they stay or go?
I didn't want to find out, I let out a pleading shout.
The ghost girl turned, my stomach churned.
She ran back and headed on track
And cantered off into the horizon.

*Yasmin Welham (11)*
*North & South Cowton Primary School*


## AT THE ZOO

The monkey jumped up a tree,
He was having fun.
The lion growled at the keeper
Because he took away his son.
The bear was very angry
Because he was stuck in a cage.
The snake slithered through the grass
With his slimy skin he goes along.
The elephant squirts water,
The giraffe waves his neck.

*Louise Pearson (9)*
*North & South Cowton Primary School*

## DOLPHINS

We swim together through the sea.
Diving through the waves
They come and see me.

We chase up and down
Through the glistening fish,
I glide on the dolphin's back.
As the night falls,
We say goodbye.

I ride off in the boat,
The dolphin flapping its flippers
As we sail home.

*Abby Weighell (9)*
*North & South Cowton Primary School*


## WATERFALLS

Water crashing on the rocks,
Smashing boulders to pieces,
Gushing onto the sand.
The fish try to jump,
The water slams them down.
The water drowns a deer
Drinking from the lake.
When the waterfall calms down,
More animals come to drink.
They like it better when it's calm,
They can catch the fish in peace.

*Dexter Turner (8)*
*North & South Cowton Primary School*

## THE SHIP

The ship rocks and rolls,
It sways from side to side,
It has huge funnels.

The ship travels
From far and near,
Land to land,
Country to country.

When the anchor sinks
Down into the seabed,
It goes to sleep.

*James Donaldson (8)*
*North & South Cowton Primary School*


## DOGS

Some dogs are fat
And others are thin.
Some dogs are cuddly
And some like to win.
Some dogs like to lick
And others like to play.
Some like to be kissed
And some sleep all day.
Some dogs are so greedy
And always pinch food.
My dog tends to frown,
But he's never in a mood.

*Daisy Shaw (8)*
*North & South Cowton Primary School*

## THE KILLER GHOST!

He is not ordinary, he is different.
He is not white, he is black and red,
Black to show his life's darkness
And red for the blood to show how he was killed.
He carries big, heavy chains to scare people,
Until they are as pale as pale can get,
And then he pulls out his butcher's knife and kills them.
The blade is red and clotted with blood.
Nobody knows why he does it, maybe for fun,
Or maybe to get back at the person who killed him.
So watch your backs, be careful how you sleep,
Because maybe, just maybe, he could come to you!

*Raegan Shaw (9)*
*North & South Cowton Primary School*


## SUMMER WIND

The summer wind blows blossom down,
The sun shines brightly,
Birds sing and twitter sweetly,
Summer wind strokes a dancing tree,
Makes the water ripple.
I play and shout,
But as night draws on,
I know it is the last day of summer.

*Bethany Wilson (8)*
*North & South Cowton Primary School*

## My Mum Said . . .

My mum said I couldn't go out to play,
But I forgot
And did anyway.
My mum said not to ruin my shirt,
But I forgot
And it's covered in dirt.
My mum said to answer the phone,
But I forgot,
She started to moan.
My mum said to come for tea,
But I forgot
Till ten to three.
Then my dad said, 'I have a present for you.'
But this time I didn't forget,
I tell you, it's true.

*Stacey Robson (11)*
*Romanby Primary School*


## My Old, Crooked Granny

My old, crooked granny is coming to stay,
She'll bring old stories and tales, hooray!
All she wants is a cup of tea,
My mum won't listen and she blames it on me.
She bought me a teddy, I like it a lot,
A dead, scruffy plant was all my mum got.
She sits on her chair, in front of the fire,
Into her bed, she soon will retire.
My old, crooked granny is coming to stay,
She'll bring . . .

*Ellis Hayes (9)*
*Romanby Primary School*

## THE CITY BEAR

It was a cold, dark night,
With a cold, dark air
And on a little city street
There was a great big bear!

It escaped from the zoo
By jumping over bars,
Then ran around the city
And trampled on cars!

In the morning it was found
Sleeping on the green,
But no one dared approach it
Because it looked so mean!

The RSPCA came
And took it far away,
But no one will forget
What happened on that day.

*Matthew Codd (10)*
*Romanby Primary School*


## FEELINGS POEM

Afraid is a very dark cave,
Full of vampires, ghosts and bats,
And quiet voices whispering, 'Give me blood,'
Lonely sewers and rats.

Bored is sad and unhappy faces
And toys all locked in a cupboard,
An empty, silent room,
With no one to be seen.

Grumpy is angry and mad,
Boiling up inside like a
Red, fiery dragon and turning
White-hot, like a sheet of A4 paper.

*Jamie Kirby (11)*
*Romanby Primary School*

## ANGER

Anger is a fiery dragon,
Burning everything in sight.
The forests all turn to ashes
As anger takes flight.

When my dad gets really mad
Because he's late for work
And all the traffic lights are red,
He storms and honks his horn!

When my mum has a baking day
And all her cakes are flops,
She rants and raves and smoke comes from
Her nose and ears and mouth!

And during all this great upset,
I hide under my bed.
Then in the morning the dragon dies
And everything's peaceful again.

*Sebastian Rab (10)*
*Romanby Primary School*

## FARMING PROBLEMS

Farmers of both kinds are amazing,
Arable and animal.
It's admirable how they coped
With all of their problems.

You see when foot and mouth came,
What an awful state,
This wouldn't go quickly at any rate.
But there's still meat in Tesco,
We can still eat al fresco
And that's because they still pressed on.

They kept on growing vegetables when the reservoir was dry,
They kept digging them up and we still had carrot pie,
And that's because they still pressed on.

Even when the bugs ate their crops,
They stood firm, didn't lose their tops,
Used a little pesticide and kept producing food.

***Richard Hounsome (11)***
***Romanby Primary School***


## WHY SHOULD I?

My mum said, 'Do your homework!'
Do my homework? Why should I?
I'm going out to play, or I will cry!
It's got to be in on Monday, so why should I?

My dad said, 'Fetch the remote controls!'
Fetch the remote controls? Why should I?
I want to watch TV, or I will pout!
It's my favourite programme now, so why should I?

My sister said, 'Play with me!'
Play with her? Why should I?
I'm playing with the cat, or I'll be sick!
The kitten is wide awake now, so why should I?

My kitten said, 'Pick me up!'
Pick her up? Why should I?
I have to read a book for school or I'll be in trouble!
It's a good book, so why should I?

*Grace Kirk (9)*
*Romanby Primary School*


## GRAVEYARD

Once there lived a man called Peter Hogg,
Stabbed to death by his little pet frog.

Once there lived a man called Freddy McLung,
Ate a sucky sweet and swallowed his tongue.

Once there lived a man called Derek Pratt,
Shot to death by his furry pet cat.

Once there lived a man called Billy Voice,
Strangled to death by his old auntie Joyce.

Once there lived a man called Richard Bake,
Poisoned to death by his old pet snake.

Once there lived a man called Jonathan Curd,
Pushed off a cliff by his large pet bird.

Once there lived a man called . . .

*James Lacy (10)*
*Romanby Primary School*

## No!

My dad said,
'Don't moan and get me the phone!
Eat your dinner and be much quicker!
Don't scowl and bring me a towel!'

My mum said,
'Don't sit there and smirk, do your homework!
Tidy your room or else I will hit you with a broom!
Don't give me grief, just brush your teeth!'

I said,
*'No!'*

*Joe Clarkson (10)*
*Romanby Primary School*


## Night-Time Wonders

At night-time in my bed,
I have pictures in my head.
Sometimes horses, sometimes wings,
Sometimes very nasty things.
It all comes together in a way,
A way I cannot say.
You'll find out soon, when you have that dream,
That dream of wonders waiting to be dreamed.

*Lindsay Walker (8)*
*St Cuthbert's Primary School, Pateley Bridge*

## TODAY, YESTERDAY AND TOMORROW

Today
I walked into class.
Miss Kaye was scrubbing out some numbers.
I sat next to a girl who had just snapped her lead.
I put my bag down
And watched the fish
Floating backwards and forwards.

Yesterday
I gurgled over a book cover
And slavered on its pages.
I dialled 999 and said,
'Faslabaslastah.'
Staring out of the window,
Looking up at the sky . . .

Tomorrow,
I will wake up and look at the time,
I will rush into my car,
I will scurry into work
With my hair ruffled.
I will quickly return to my car,
Look in the mirror,
Run into my home
And decide I should stop at home,
Then I will have a drink of wine.

*Jasmine Briggs (8)*
*St Hilda's RC Primary School, Whitby*

## STORMY NIGHT

Skies flashing,
Trees falling,
Zigzags in the sky.
Babies wailing,
Mums shouting,
Rain falling on the window,
Doors banging,
Roof tiles flying around.
The Devil's grumble
I can hear . . .
I do hope the sun is near.

*Magnus McAuley (9)*
*St Hilda's RC Primary School, Whitby*


## SUNNY

Sun bright
Shining down at me
As it bursts into flames.
Then the rain comes,
Sad
As I go in.
Trying to be happiest,
Then the sun comes,
Now I am happy
As I go out to play.

*Josie Wilkinson (8)*
*St Hilda's RC Primary School, Whitby*

## THE SUNNY DAY

The sun blazing across flowers,
The clouds fading away,
The sky turning blue.
The hot, fiery sun, shining away on the cool swimming pool,
The bright glittering flowers, shining across the pool.
People putting sun cream on,
The hot dazzling sun
Burning the bright sky up.

*Marcia Kipling (8)*
*St Hilda's RC Primary School, Whitby*


## STORMY DAYS

Thunder clouds lighting the sky and
Shooting stars shooting across the sky.
Forked lightning flying
And power cuts in people's houses.
Bricks smashing windows.

*Francesca Roe (8)*
*St Hilda's RC Primary School, Whitby*


## MY PSALM

Let the moon light up,
Like a thousand diamonds
That join up in a flash,
With a sparkle of dust,
Just like a clock ticking away.

*Francis Clark (8)*
*St Hilda's RC Primary School, Whitby*

## A Dark And Stormy Night

*Bang,*
*Clatter,*
*Bang,*
*Clatter,*
It's a windy night.

It's raining,
*Drip,*
*Drop,*
Against the window.

We are shocked,
In fright,
Cars are crashing because of the fog.
Floorboards are creaking through the night,
Again we are
*Shocked,*
*In*
*Fright!*

***Frances Wright (8)***
***St Hilda's RC Primary School, Whitby***


## Sunny

The sunshine sprinkles on my flowers,
But thank you, Lord, for not giving me showers.

The birds squawk,
But we walk and talk.

Now the rain comes gain,
Then the sun trots along the lane,
So I go home to play again.

***Amy Pearson (9)***
***St Hilda's RC Primary School, Whitby***

## THE STORM

Lightning is flashing all around,
People are petrified.
Inside people's houses their lights are flashing.
On their roofs,
Tiles move
And wobble,
To and fro.

The birds crash into the walls,
Windows,
Birds hide in their nests
And trees
Wobble
To and fro.

*Frances Cairns (8)*
*St Hilda's RC Primary School, Whitby*


## STORMY WEATHER

Lightning appears from the sky,
But the chilly frost is nearby.
Before it is raw,
Before it is sharp,
Inside I am playing the harp.
The lightning rises again from the sky,
But still the frost is nearby.
Before, we play,
Before, we have fun,
Now we wait for the sun to come.

*Kirstie Lloyd (8)*
*St Hilda's RC Primary School, Whitby*

## A STORMY NIGHT

Trees waving from side to side,
Sea crashing against the sharp cliffs,
Furious winds lifting roofs off house tops,
Lighting -
Flashing,
Zipping and zapping.
Wind going crazy in the sky.

*Rikki Roach (9)*
*St Hilda's RC Primary School, Whitby*


## HIDDEN TREASURES

H　orizon clutches a desert island,
I　nstead of
D　esertion turns to
D　anger,
E　xotic birds roam the skies,
N　ever will the

T　reassures lie.
R　agged pirate comes to land,
E　nchantment spreads through,
A　nimals flee the island,
S　ecrets scatter in the open air,
U　ncaring pirates
R　un to the enchanted gold,
E　nergetic sailors
S　ave the day.

*James Howe (10)*
*St Martin's CE Aided Primary School, Scarborough*

## CARS

C onvertible,
A n estate,
R acing cars,
S ports cars.

R acing,
A ll courses hard,
L iking every metre,
L and not level,
Y elling co-drivers.

M otor,
O ver hills
T o race,
O verturned cars,
S uspension gone,
P it stop,
O pening bonnet,
R unning to pit,
T he race won.

*Richard Walker (10)*
*St Martin's CE Aided Primary School, Scarborough*

## FOOTBALL

*F*ootball is
*O*ne
*O*f
*T*he
*B*est
*GA*mes I
*L*ove
*PL*aying it.

*Jonathan Corrie (10)*
*St Martin's CE Aided Primary School, Scarborough*

### TREASURES

Glittering old, spell-binding to all,
Its mysterious power controlling all.

Supreme silver has driven people to the ends of the Earth,
Telling everyone to go to the mine, find me.

Perfect platinum, the most valuable thing ever to be made,
Deep in the ocean will man go, here for perfect platinum.

Desperate diamonds, a girl's best friend.
This jewel is more than a wedding gesture,
But a sign of eternal love.

But the treasure that is most important to me
Is love!

*Ben Smith (10)*
*St Martin's CE Aided Primary School, Scarborough*


### BROWN

Hazelnut brown, the crackling bark on a tree,
Squelching, muddy country footpath,
Towering wall about to fall.
Two colliding conkers, shining brown, glistening.
Autumn leaves like crumpled brown paper,
All crinkled and ready to fall.

*Robert Squire (10)*
*St Martin's CE Aided Primary School, Scarborough*

## THE BLACKNESS

The park was old and dark
And the trees had reaching arms,
As if trying to catch me.
The old pub was in total blackness
As shadowy figures scuttled along.

There stood a church and behind that, a path.
The path was creepy and all crumbling up,
Then out of the dark came a beach.
I could hear the waves
Crashing against the rocks,
Like a raging fire
As the wind whistled, ear-splitting, through the trees.

The beach was sandy
With smooth stones scattered here and there.
Suddenly all was light!
Out of the dark came a beautiful sight
And I could see all around myself.

But nobody was there.
A wave swept over the sky
Like a large beast,
Then all was dark,
For I had been dragged into the sea.

*Annie O'Sullivan (9)*
*St Martin's CE Aided Primary School, Scarborough*

## THE RAPPIN' PIRATES OF THE SEA

The ship was rotten, scary and old,
Up on board the air was cold
And the pirates gathered around the map,
There and then they began to rap.
'Oh we're the rappin' pirates of the sea,
Come down 'ere and listen to me.
We've got this map to find our gold,
That'll keep us going till we're old.
On this map, 'X' marks the spot,
We'll keep on diggin' till we've got the lot.'
For a year and a day they sailed on,
It seemed that all their dreams were gone.
'Excuse me Captain, I can't cope,
I haven't got that much hope.'
Until the skipper spotted land
And all the pirates waved their hands.
Oh, the rappin' pirates will now dig,
'Cast off that sail and pull the rig.'
With a shove and a spade,
(and a hand grenade)
But then they started to wreck the ground.
Cattle and sheep were prancing around
As the pirates drilled and blocked a hole.
They ruined homes, the worms, the mole.
The mole he was a fantastic rapper,
So they rapped and they rapped
And the dug and they dug until,
*Gold!* And they gave a big tug.
'Get this box o' jewels outta here,
Those robbers must be very near.'

***Rosie O'Sullivan (10)***
***St Martin's CE Aided Primary School, Scarborough***

## HIDDEN TREASURE

H idden treasure at the bottom of the sea,
I n a sunken ship.
D ivers try to find the gems and jewels,
D eep, deep, at the bottom of the sea.
E very diamond hidden away,
N ever to be found.

R olling in the current,
I ncredible rubies red and green,
C ooked in the ocean,
H ighly treasured among women and men,
E ngraved in the sand,
S oon will be found.

*James Aitchison (10)*
*St Martin's CE Aided Primary School, Scarborough*


## THE ELEPHANT

Big as a bungalow, big as a bus,
As it comes, it makes a sound like a lorry falling from above.
Its skin is like an old Roman floor and crumpled bricks,
Ears like big round satellite dishes.
Tail swings from side to side like a pendulum clock,
Legs brush through the long grass like bulldozers.
Dull eyes look like they're never going to blink,
Trunk like a big brass trumpet.
Nothing in its way, it walks on then, gone . . .

*Samuel Tindall (10)*
*St Martin's CE Aided Primary School, Scarborough*

## PIRATES

In 1533 the gentlemen of pirates got their fortunes.
The Spanish ships' greatest fear were pirates seeking their fortunes.
Sea battles were common, started by the men seeking their fortunes!

Seeking their fortunes, ruthless pirates,
Killing for treasure, horrible pirates,
Digging for treasure, battling pirates!

Pirates' cutlasses and pistols,
Men dying from fire and pistols,
Short firearms, pirates' pistols!

Pistols firing, men falling over a treasure chest,
Burying their overflowing chest,
Staying hidden for thousands of years, the treasure chest!

The treasure chest aboard a Spanish ship,
Creeping up, the smaller pirate ship,
Heavy cannonballs could sink either ship!

Ship of Spanish soldiers operating a large cannon,
Deck and hull creaking under the large cannon,
Ships falling to the large cannon!

Cannon fire resulting in skeletons,
Men dying, leaving skeletons,
Leg bones lying around from broken skeletons!

Skeletons of brave, but dead men,
Treasure seekers, pirates and Spanish men,
Archaeologists digging for the treasures of ancient men!

Men of great likeness of heroes,
Henry Morgan an English hero,
But all too often dead was the hero!

Heroes of the Caribbean,
Villains of the Caribbean,
But pirate haven the Caribbean!

*Robert Mead (9)*
*St Martin's CE Aided Primary School, Scarborough*


## HIDDEN TREASURES

H  idden treasure
I   n a
D  eserted ship and
D  estroyed, nobody has
E  ven found a golden jewel,
N  ot even a golden brooch.

T  reasure lays beneath the sea,
R  esting right at the bottom of the deep blue sea,
E  verybody tries to find it
A  nd search for the map,
S  earching
U  nder the sea,
R  eally precious to you and me and
E  very pirate too.

*Charlotte Harrison (10)*
*St Martin's CE Aided Primary School, Scarborough*

## THE DAFFODIL

Imagine a daffodil all on its own,
Standing freely, but all alone,
With its long face hanging down.
It looks to me like a frown.

The daffodil is sad,
He's also lonely.
He swings back and forth
In the blustery wind.

'I have no friends,
Except for Poppy.
She's really nice,
But it's me she copies.

I've got a big red nose
And bluefish eyes,
I smile when I'm happy,
But frown when I'm sad.'

Imagine a daffodil, all on its own,
Standing freely, but all alone,
With its long face hanging down,
It still looks to me like a frown.

*Alicia Salt (10)*
*St Nicholas CE Primary School, Ripon*

## IT'S JUST ANOTHER DAY

We arrive in the playground,
It's pouring down with rain.
All my friends are moaning
Because we can't play football again.

We go into the classroom,
We have a spelling test.
I struggled learning them at home,
But I'll just have to try my best.

Very soon it's playtime,
We have to stay in class,
We are really disappointed,
We would rather play on the grass.

Maths is next, we all sit down
And look out of the window.
I cannot believe it! There's the sun
And over there's a rainbow.

We can't wait till home time.
When the bell rings, we'll all run out.
At last the weekend has arrived,
It's time to sing and shout.

*Steven Durrans (10)*
*St Nicholas CE Primary School, Ripon*

## The Aliens

The aliens are coming,
Some are fat, some slim.
What will they do when they get here?
What will they travel in?
The aliens are coming.

The aliens are coming closer.
Are they nasty or are they kind?
Will they have some fiendish plot?
When they get here, what will they find?
The aliens are coming closer.

The aliens are here.
Will they have weapons or not?
The aliens are here.

The aliens have stopped.
Why is this? I don't know why.
Look, over there, up in the sky . . .
What is it? Where is it from?
The aliens have stopped.

The aliens are going,
The aliens are going.
Was it a dream?
Were they real, these things I've seen?
The aliens have gone.

*Sam Watkins (10)*
*St Nicholas CE Primary School, Ripon*

## MY DREAM CAR

My dream car would be a Dodge Viper,
A car for everyone to see.
Of course, its colours are really important,
Especially for me.

Well, if I couldn't have that,
I would have a Ferrari F50 with its V8 petrol engine.
Just listen to the sound of its roaring,
Well, I like my dream cars.

But, if I couldn't have that,
Then I would have a Porsche 911.
The colour, well, it would be black and the alloys,
Well, they would be gold.
I like my dream cars.

Someday I will get my dream car,
But until then,
I'll just have to wait.
But, I like my dream cars.

*Ben Ambler (11)*
*St Nicholas CE Primary School, Ripon*

## THE MIST

The mist crept
While I slept.

The mist crept
Through the shadows
In the meadows.

The mist crept
While I slept.

*Emma Scott (9)*
*St Nicholas CE Primary School, Ripon*

## IF I HAD A BEST FRIEND

If I had a best friend, she would probably be silly,
If she had some sisters, her best one would be called Millie.
Her hobby would be to keep fit and go to the gym,
She'd like to go to school, but she'd be a bit dim.

She'd be a bit of a clown,
She'd be so silly she might go swimming in her dressing gown,
And she'd be brill at sums,
But when she's counting, she'll use her thumbs.

Sometimes she might be quick
Other times, she'd make people sick!
She might even have a house full of pets,
But with all the food, it would give her some debts.

She might like to read a lot of books,
With all the pets, she might have a pond full of ducks.
She might even chat to me on the phone,
While one of her dogs chews a bone.

*Jessie Perry (11)*
*St Nicholas CE Primary School, Ripon*


## BUTTERFLIES

Butterflies are beautiful,
If I was a butterfly
I would fly all day
Till I got tired.
If I was a butterfly
I would love my colours.
I like butterflies,
I like the colours.

Butterflies mostly
Come out at summer
When it is warm.
I see, I see
Butterflies all around me,
And different colours
All around me too.

*Stefania Finch (8)*
*St Wilfrid's RC Primary School, York*


## THE CAT

Miaow, I am the cat
Slinking through the alley,
Prancing past houses and trees,
For I am the cat
Coming that way.

I sometimes eat mice and birds,
And get into mischief
But I do not care,
No, for I am the cat
Coming that way.

I am heading towards you
Looking for mischief,
But I do not care . . .
No, for I am the cat
Coming that way.

I am the hunter
Coming that way,
I am heading towards you
For I am the cat,
Prrrr, coming that way.

*Isobella Turnell (7)*
*St Wilfrid's RC Primary School, York*

## MY FRIEND

My imaginary friend
likes ice cream blend,
He sits on the hay
Drinking all day,
When he sleeps
He always peeps,
And then he goes fast asleep.

My imaginary friend is very silly
Because he doesn't put a coat on when he's chilly,
Then he catches a cold and moans
And when he sneezes he groans,
My friend eats spice
And then he needs some rice.

*Keziah J Brookes (8)*
*St Wilfrid's RC Primary School, York*


## THE CLASSROOM

The legs of the tables are brown
To make the table stay round.

Mrs Lee's pen is blue,
She writes the register with it.

The literacy book is big
To make everyone see the book.

The counters are round,
We use them to play games with.

Andy Baker's pens smell of different things,
He likes the smell of the pens he's got.

*David King (7)*
*St Wilfrid's RC Primary School, York*

## MY FRIEND PHILIP BROWN

    My friend Philip Brown
    Turns my house upside-down!
    Whether it's good or whether it's bad
    He always tries to wind up my dad!

My friend Philip Brown
Follows my mum all around,
He always gets to the cookie jar
While my dad's out at the bar!

    My friend Philip Brown
    Turns my family upside-down!
    Only you and I know who
    Philip Brown is.

*Hannah Jackson (8)*
*St Wilfrid's RC Primary School, York*


## LEAVES

Leaves being pulled by the
Wind twizzling everywhere.
In autumn leaves change
Colours, red,
Yellow, orange.
So as spring comes
Everything starts to change
And all leaves are green
And on the trees again.
Winter is another story,
Leaves are frizzling
And trees are bare.

*Nicole Zannikos (8)*
*St Wilfrid's RC Primary School, York*

## COLOURS

What is green?
A witch's long, crooked nose,
The nice swaying grass,
And my thick curly hair.

What is red?
Hot volcanic ash,
My blood bursting out of my arm,
And the big red scissors snapping at me.

What is white?
The big, bony skeleton,
The very tiny TV I have to watch
And my woolly duvet.

What is silver?
Nice, smooth unicorn blood,
My metal aeroplane,
And my big lunchbox.

What is purple?
My friends sparkle sharpener,
My new flashy trainers,
And my tiny brain.

*Andy Baker (8)*
*St Wilfrid's RC Primary School, York*


## HIDDEN TREASURE

Hidden treasure is a bowl of gold,
Treasure can make you rich.
Hidden treasure sinks, sinks down
To the bottom of the deep blue sea.

Treasure is gold and silver,
Gold is a pen,
Gold is a pound coin,
I love gold.

*Nicole Vogwill (7)*
*Settrington All Saints CE Primary School*

## HIDDEN TREASURE

People think of hidden treasure like
Necklaces,
Rings,
Bangles,
Tools,
Money,
Cups, mugs,
Diamond stones,
Watches,
Dresses,
Oceans,
Ornaments
And a pirate's telescope,
But not me I think of
A shiny key hooked up on the wall,
And a shiny sword being pulled out of its case,
And I can't forget my chocolate!

*Rebecca Stubbings (11)*
*Settrington All Saints CE Primary School*

## HIDDEN TREASURE

I bet you think about,
Jewels,
Chocolate coins,
Gold necklaces,
Silver rings,
Sparkly earrings,
A handful of seaweed,
A treasure map,
Cheerful monkeys,
Scary pirates,
Huge pirate ships,
Chattering parrots,
Rattley bones,
An old bit of wood from a drowned ship,
A colourful octopus,
But not me I would think about . . .
*Chocolate!*

**Samantha Marwood (10)**
**Settrington All Saints CE Primary School**


## HIDDEN TREASURES I BET YOU THINK ABOUT

Pirates, parrots and ships,
Gold, silver, diamonds, pearls, emeralds, rubies, sapphires, garnets,
Maps, treasure chests and islands,
Crosses on the sand,
The treasure in a treasure hunt,
Booming cannonballs,
Mouldy skeletons,
Old rusty coins.

But not me, I think about . . .
Jewellery in a golden decorated box,
Chocolate truffles from Thorntons,
Henry a big chocolate bear,
A very old key in a wooden box to open a door in a tree,
Caveman paintings on a damp, brown cave wall,
One hundred different coloured pencil crayons.

*Beth Nicholson (11)*
*Settrington All Saints CE Primary School*

## HIDDEN TREASURE

I bet you think about
Silver, sparkling jewels,
Gold coins,
Two magic rings,
One-eyed pirates,
Old maps,
Bones,
Old pirate ships,
Parrots,
But not me I would like to think about,
Old torn up photos,
Old dusty books,
Sparkling watches.

*Jade Hoggard (9)*
*Settrington All Saints CE Primary School*

## HIDDEN TREASURE

Jolly monkeys,
Frightening pirates,
Scary pirate ships,
Old boxes of gold,
Crooked bones,
Chatty parrots,
A hot island,
A deep blue sea,
Cold caves,
Banging cannons,
Hungry crocodiles,
Ragged treasure map,
A black cross on the sand,
Melting candles next to the treasure,
Pirates' skulls,
Spooky jungles,
Used up eye patches,
Old beer bottles with a letter inside,
Dangerous octopus,
Slimy seaweed.

I dream of . . .
A photo of a pretty girl,
A tiny box
Buried under an oak tree,
Made by a helpful shoemaker,
Sparkly golden key,
A lock of hair from a favourite girl,
One lucky earring.

***Rosie Buckland (9)***
***Settrington All Saints CE Primary School***

## THE OLD MAN

In this biting frost
An old man crouches, shivering,
His name is Fred.
I walk over to him,
His blue lips speak not a word . . .

'Good morning, and merry Christmas,'
I said cheerfully.
There was no reply from his still lips.
We enter a shop and shop like flames
Dashing into the fire,
We walk slowly back out in the biting frost.

Our footsteps rustle softly in the sheet of snow.
Fred loses his footing, I try to grab his hand.
I miss, I dash to the shop, dial nine, nine, nine,
And shout, 'Ambulance.'

The old man, tears drip down his wrinkled face,
Clutches at his chest.
The rushing ambulance arrives,
They ask me long questions.

They carry him on a snow-covered stretcher
Into the freezing cold and I weep,
Head down and walk over to take myself home,
Tears drip on my carpet, I take off my coat
And turn on the fire, at last I fall asleep.

I wake up, I peep out of my dust-covered window,
I see old Fred in a wheelchair,
I leap outside to greet him,
He was gripping something,
Of course, it's a bag with coal in!

*Tasha Lawrance (9)*
*Thorpe Willoughby CP School*

## OLD MAN

It's a freezing cold day outside,
As white as a sheet.
Clouds dark and fields white
Like a Christmas card.

The old man shuffles his feet
Through ice and snow.
With a bag clung in his hands,
He put his head down and off he went,
He didn't have time to chatter.

In his bag was coal
But he doesn't have much,
He's left a track of footprints
While he shuffles home.

He's heading towards home
When he went down a slippery hill,
Just like a crab
To get away from the snow.

*Dale Holt  (10)*
*Thorpe Willoughby CP School*


## OLD MAN

The day is light,
The old man walked.
The day is still bright,
The old man talked.

The day is cold,
And the man is old,
Strolls along the snowy path,
Dreams about a hot bath.

I got back home
Where it's lovely and warm,
Sits near scalding heat
In his comfortable seat.

*Stephen Dean (10)*
*Thorpe Willoughby CP School*


## THE OLD MAN

He makes his way
Towards the shop on
This cold and snowy day.
He normally stops to
Talk to me but today
He's on his way.

Quickly and quietly
He gets on his way,
Not stopping to say
Hello, he will
Just keep going.
Then he arrives
At the shop and
Barely takes a minute.

He's on,
He's on his way now,
Still won't stop to chat.
He hurries back again,
Clutching a sack of coal.
He checks his watch,
I turn around and turn
Back again but he is gone.

*Cameron Robertson (9)*
*Thorpe Willoughby CP School*

## OLD MAN

The cold glittery winter's day,
Icy drops hanging from frosty houses,
Sparkling like burning flames,
The snow crackling beneath his feet.

Warm air drifting out of his frosted mouth,
Trying to warm his hands,
Shivering like an iceberg,
Gripping tightly to his bag,
Walking step by step.

Getting faster and faster,
Nearly running,
He usually stops and talks to people,
Not this time though.

Getting smaller and smaller,
Nearly collapsing in the snow,
The old man trembling home,
Starting to turn the fire on,
With red, yellow, orange and blue flames
Flying in the air, bringing smoky colours off it.

*Natalie Carse (11)*
*Thorpe Willoughby CP School*


## OLD MAN

On a dark and gloomy day
The old man stumbles on,
Gripping tightly to his coal bag,
Leaving a trail of footmarks behind.

As the snow keeps falling down
On the poor and lonely man,
He breathes out sparkly smoke
To keep him very warm.

Usually he has a chat to me
But this time he ignored me.
As he's walking faster and faster
He finally reaches the door.

He pants with relief
As he gets in the door,
And turns the fire on with bright and colourful flames,
Then sits down and relaxes with a cup of tea.

*Adam Carse (11)*
*Thorpe Willoughby CP School*

## OLD MAN

On this cold icy day
The old man goes walking,
Clutching a bulging bag.

As he wobbled down the way
The snow falls all around,
The only sound is the clip of the horses' hooves.

His hands are held high,
His breath is white like fog
As he stumbled home.

His tight lips say no words
As he heads towards his refuge
When I try to talk to him.

When he arrives at his refuge
He places the coal from the bulging bag on the fire,
Then puts on the kettle for a warm drink.

*Katie Matthews (10)*
*Thorpe Willoughby CP School*

## OLD MAN

An old man walking through the huge snowflake,
He walks like a giant through the deep, deep snow,
Lifting his feet from the ground.

Gripping tightly he holds a bag to his chest,
I wonder what it is,
It must be something to keep him going
In this cold, cold weather.

It must be important if he's holding it tight,
No words pass his lips, as people stop to talk,
No mutter or a breath comes out of his lips.

All he does is walk straight past them then disappear
Into the misty fog,
He is nearly home, he slides to his door,
Turns his key and goes inside,
Slips off his boots, takes his coat off,
Turns his fire on and gets a cup of tea.

*Rebecca Yould (11)*
*Thorpe Willoughby CP School*


## OLD MAN

On this bitter freezing day
The old man trudges over the ice,
He wobbles but keeps his balance
By a crumple red bag
Clasped to his chest.

As he skids and slides to get home
To an arctic house,
As his body gets colder,
His eyes light up, brighter than blazes.

When he reaches his humble abode
He sits in front of the fire,
And puts the bag on the black screen,
And lights it with matches from his pocket.

*Sam Grinsill (10)*
*Thorpe Willoughby CP School*

## OLD MAN

On this very cold winter's day
The snow is falling heavily,
You can't see the ground
Because it's full of snow,
He needs to go to the shop
To buy a bag of coal.

He looked very cold even though
He had his hat on, his scarf
And gloves on too.
Then he reached the shop door,
Opened it and said,
'It's warm in here,'
Then he shut the door again.

When he came out of the shop
He was clutching on to a bag
And walking off slowly home.
When he got to his house
He opened the door.

An hour later I knocked on the door,
And he answered,
'Can you come round tomorrow
Afternoon because at the moment
I'm too busy?'

*Stacey Welbourn (10)*
*Thorpe Willoughby CP School*

## OLD MAN

It is a frosty evening
And the cold winds were blowing,
The trees are rustling,
The wind is whistling.

The old man wraps up in his itchy clothes,
Trying to keep warm and dry,
His hands are climbing up his coat.

He clenches his hands to the bag he is carrying,
The coal in the grey, silky bag,
Just for warmth.

The puff of steam storming
From his mouth,
His eyes trying to stay open.

His teeth tightening together,
His legs shaking, trying to get
Through the white snow.

He finally arrives at his wet door,
He stumbles to the fire and lights it.

It turns blue and red,
He snuggles down into his cosy bed.

*Leanne Walker (11)*
*Thorpe Willoughby CP School*

## THE OLD MAN

It is a cold snowy day and the old man is out
Doing his everyday shopping.
There he is shuffling his feet through the thick snow
As he puffs steam out into the cold winter's air.

He hobbles down the footpath and returns with a bag of coal,
As he clenches on to it
He walks slowly but gradually back
So he can warm up.

It is now three o'clock and the old man is nice and warm inside
Next to the warm fire with a cat beside.

*William McVittie (9)*
*Thorpe Willoughby CP School*

## OLD MAN

I walked past
The old man,
He didn't say a word,
He walked straight
Past me clutching
Tight a bag of coal,
Looking sorry for
Himself, sliding
Through the
Tough, treacherous
Snow that
This day has
Brought,
As he gets
Home he
Lights the
Fire, he
Loves the heat
Of the open hearth.

*Adam Taylor (9)*
*Thorpe Willoughby CP School*

## OLD MAN

This cold bitter morning
The old man is struggling to get home,
His head down, walking very slowly,
He is wrapped up warm in a coat and hat.

This freezing icy morning,
Gripping a bag like it holds his life,
He struggles to move being so cautious,
As he moves his determination grows.

This snowy morning,
His home is near, the journey almost over,
The man shows no intention of stopping.

Almost over he looks back at his path,
He gets his keys, opens the door
And heads straight to the fire,
Still gripping the bag,
He turns it on, takes off his coat
And settles down for the night.

*Tom Rich  (10)*
*Thorpe Willoughby CP School*


## OLD MAN

On this cold and snowy day
He hurries on his way,
With his head down
And a coal bag in his hand.

He hurries straight past me,
Never said hello.
He struggles on with the bag in his hand,
Walking along like a one man band.

Puffing out steam like an engine
Transporting the coal to a scorching hot fire.
Arriving home to a boiling kettle
And puts his feet up against the fire.

*Jack Greenwood (9)*
*Thorpe Willoughby CP School*

## THE OLD MAN

Chilly and frosty it is today,
This slippery and icy floor.
This old man crouches and shivers,
His hands all shiver and shake.
A tiny bag of coal close to chest,
That's all he could afford.

This cold and chilly day
His feet could not stay still,
He mumbles as he slowly strolls on
With his feet sinking in the snow,
He slowly pulls his feet out of the snow.

He has little time to stand and chat,
He has to make his way home,
His frosty boots tramp on.

He turns slowly to head for home,
He decides to put the bag in his cold coat,
He tries hard to fight this chilly day,
His eyes almost water because of all this snow.

*Hayley Pallett (9)*
*Thorpe Willoughby CP School*

## THE OLD MAN

The old man is crunched
Up in a corner with
A bag held like a little child
Clutching his teddy bear.
I walked up to him,
He was shaking like
A tree in a strong wind.

He's normally chatty,
But he didn't even say a word to me.
I can feel he's thinking about something.
He starts to walk to his house.

I think when he gets home
He will put on his fire
And have a hot drink.

***Christopher Allen (11)***
***Thorpe Willoughby CP School***


## OLD MAN

On a cold and bitter day,
Gilderoy who is usually chattery
Just walks past his friends,
As he trudges on his way,
Struggling to take one more foot
Through the mountain deep snow.

Gilderoy is old and creaky,
As he tries to rush, nothing happens,
He just plods on.
He has hair the colour of snow,
His nose is cold and his eyes aglow.

He grips a small bag in his gloved hands,
Head down, thinking of the warm home
He will return to,
And he will leave the dreadful weather outside.

*Danielle Amos (10)*
*Thorpe Willoughby CP School*


## OLD MAN

This cold bitter morning,
An old man was scuttling home.
This cold bitter morning,
An old man walking alone.

This cold bitter morning,
Snow falling to the ground.
This cold bitter morning,
Frozen ground all around.

This cold bitter morning,
A man in gloves, scarf and hat.
This cold bitter morning,
He must get home, no time to chat.

This cold bitter morning,
A man gripping a bag of coal.
This cold bitter morning,
It was as snowy as the North Pole.

This cold bitter morning,
In the place he loves best.
This cold bitter morning,
In the warmth, having a rest.

*Jennifer Raechel Carter (10)*
*Thorpe Willoughby CP School*

# OLD MAN

A cold winter's day,
Snow motionless on
The garden path.
Ice on the road like
A giant snow scene.

An old man walks
Out the door, bags
Under his warm eyes.
He walks slowly with
Great care and trembles
Under the cold, his
Skin like plastic bags.

No time to chat,
No time to lose,
The old man steadily
Walks to the shops.
He bends to trap the
Warmth and keep cosy.

Walking back he grasps
A bag of coal, to put
In the cosy, dancing fire,
All the way back
To where no place
Is better . . . home.

*Jake Lount (11)*
*Thorpe Willoughby CP School*

## OLD MAN

It is a frosty winter's morning,
The man walks slowly on his way to the shop
With his head down and hands clenched,
He shivers and his teeth chatter on this frosty winter's day.

He passes people but keeps his lips sealed,
He gets to the shop and buys some coal,
He clenches the bag with his cold, cold hands
As he walks home.

He passes many houses and gets to his front door,
He lifts the key out of his pocket and opens the door,
He stands next to the fire rubbing his hands warm.

*Louise Jackson (10)*
*Thorpe Willoughby CP School*


## LINTON FALLS

Standing still, silent, watching the shimmering ripples
As the sun shines down on the peaceful river.

The roaring falls crash down on the river as the sound
Runs down and through the valley.

It is hard to believe that this relaxing, peaceful, calm place
Would have been a noisy, smelly, oily place
Full of hardworking men and women.

I look across the beautiful green countryside,
I hear animals and feel peaceful,
I smell the countryside air.

*Natasha Cahill (10)*
*Threshfield Primary School*

## THE PLAYGROUND

Up on Threshfield Primary School's playground
Winds blow and leaves fall,
Birds fly up in the sky
While the mist covers the trees in the distance.

Children play football in the playground,
As a penalty goes in
People cheer and run around clapping,
The whistle blows.

Once long ago the playground was rubble,
There was no football nets to play with,
Teachers were strict
With a ruler or canes.

Today in the playground people work
While teachers teach lessons.
The cloakroom is packed with coats
And the school playground is dead.

***Harry Bullough (10)***
***Threshfield Primary School***


## THE WOODS

Up in the woods, an owl flies,
Like a soaring star.
A mouse is hiding and shaking,
The moon begins to rise.

A hunter shoots a fox,
The sound is deafening.
The whistle of the wind
Sounds like the howling of dogs.

Long ago the wood wasn't here,
It was someone's dream
That became a reality,
In a green, damp patch.

*Emma Ferguson (10)*
*Threshfield Primary School*

## YARNBURY MOOR

Walking round Yarnbury Moor
Watching rabbits hopping joyfully,
Nibbling grass as they go,
Little fluffy tails bobbing in and out of view.

Walking round Yarnbury Moor
Trees swaying gently in the wind,
Holding birds, brown, grey and black,
Chirping chicks waiting hungrily for their tea.

In the past of Yarnbury Moor,
Hunters waiting, ready to pounce
Like a cat, killing a mouse,
Rabbit pie cooked and ready to eat.

Walking round Yarnbury Moor,
Lambs calling out for their mothers,
Mothers calling back to their lambs,
Running to be reunited with them.

*Rosanna Booth (9)*
*Threshfield Primary School*

## THE MOON

The moon is a pale banana
Lying in a black fruit bowl.
It is a golden C
Painted in the sky.
The moon is a baby's cot
Rocking in a dark room.
It is a rowing boat
Sailing on the sea.

The moon is a smile
Upon a dark face.
It is a round clock
Hanging on a black wall.

*Monica Yeadon (7)*
*Threshfield Primary School*


## THE MOON

The moon is an elephant's tusk
On its grey body.

It is a handle
On a dark cup.

The moon is a curly C
Written on a dark piece of paper.

It is a bright necklace
On a dark neck.

The moon is a sparkling headband
On a dark head of hair.

*Ruth Anderson (9)*
*Threshfield Primary School*

## SCHOOL DAY

Monday morning, gotta get fed,
Oh I don't wanna get out of bed,
Not another day of boring school,
It is so not very cool!

Don't like teacher Mrs Fenn,
Ohh! Not boring maths again,
PE lesson, football outside,
It was so hot, I nearly fried!

Phew it's break time, *I'm so glad!*
Gotta do lines I'm really mad!
So annoyed wanted to roar,
The entrance hall is such a bore.

Yahoo! The bell has gone at last,
Yes! I'm outta here mega fast!
Going through the cloakroom it's like a stampede!
I'm so glad to be freed!

Running down the street fast as I can,
Oops, knocked over little Dan.
Here comes his dad, big and strong,
Oh dear, oh no *Biff! Bash! Bong!*

School is over for another day,
Good tomorrow's a bank holiday,
Lying on the sofa watching TV,
I'm so glad it's all over for me.

**Simon Barnes (10)**
**Wilberfoss CE Primary School**

## LEAVES LIKE CEREALS

Leaves that are crackly like cereal without milk,
Running around like people in a shower, undressed.
Adorable dogs chasing them around the block,
Chasing leaves what next?
Now the craze is conkers,
I play it too.
Fog all over, no wonder I hear an ambulance
At a nearby crash.
How is fog made?
It drives me mad.
I would say the best thing about autumn is
Kicking the dry autumn leaves.

*Samuel Blunt (8)*
*Wilberfoss CE Primary School*


## WARM SUMMER'S DAY

One warm summer's day
I found a little buttercup
Drooping and as dry as a Rice Krispie
Without any milk,
I gave it water so it could live again.
My dad got the paddling pool out.
The morning was really warm,
Not a single cloud in the sky,
A cool breeze blew through the summer air.
I lay on the grass,
It was like swimming in a bath.
My sister and I ran round the garden.

*Amy Pack (8)*
*Wilberfoss CE Primary School*

## THE LAST OF THE WINTER HOLS

In spring there are lots of fun things,
End of the snowy Christmas holiday,
I love the yummy scrapings of the Christmas pud,
Going to a New Year's party,
Then we danced all night!
But that morning back to school,
Walking on the muddy path,
Trailing mud into the school.
Sun comes out happily,
We go outside to play,
Here comes the pouring rain,
But the sun carries on shining,
A rainbow appears in the sky.

*Georgina Warren-Porter (8)*
*Wilberfoss CE Primary School*


## WINTER HAS GONE

I think spring is a good time of year,
Other people say it isn't.
The rain in spring is beautiful and cool,
Plants start to bloom.
The evenings are getting lighter,
Leaves are growing on trees,
Animals are having babies,
And cows are making cheese.
In spring there's lots of rain,
Toddlers go out with their mums and dads.
A favourite thing of all is to jump in really big puddles!

*Alex Mercer (7)*
*Wilberfoss CE Primary School*

## ON MY OWN IN THE WOODS

In autumn leaves fall,
Some go crunch like conkers crack.
Berries burst like balloons popping,
Green ones are like stones rolling.
In the morning when I get up
I go outside to have a look,
Dawn is normally misty like smoke.
In autumn the trees are bare,
Sometimes they are grey,
But mostly they're brown.
Soon when birds make their nests
They pull big sticks to make twigs,
For their new year home.
There are clouds in the air
Waiting for the wind to blow them away,
But today the sky was cloudless.

*Charlton Wilson (7)*
*Wilberfoss CE Primary School*


## HOT SUMMER DAY

The sun comes out at summertime,
It's boiling hot on Sundays,
When you come out to play the sun will always be there.
Flowers are growing,
There're red flowers,
And yellow ones,
Purple ones too,
The cold ice cube in the drink cools me down
On hot summer days.

*Courtney Rossiter (8)*
*Wilberfoss CE Primary School*

## A Different Autumn

One autumn it was much different,
The leaves were crumbly brown,
Yellow and orange.
Grass was wet and frosty.
The ground was hard.
Conkers were ripe and squirrels were collecting.
I stepped out of the door
And the shock of mist came in.
I called my brother and sister to come
And play in the leaves.
The ground was a bit icy,
But I was in my dressing gown!
Autumn is my favourite time of year.
I had breakfast,
Then got my wellies and started to rake up the leaves,
Some trees looked very unhappy.
My brother said Jack Frost was here,
But I did not believe him.
Just then the sky looked pale blue,
Then I remembered it was the last day of autumn.

*Andrew Healey (7)*
*Wilberfoss CE Primary School*


## Sun, Sunny Day

Summer is scorching hot,
The sun is shiny orange and bright,
Plants start to droop,
It starts to go dry,
The sky is cloudless,
The wind blows faintly.

*Megan Hugill (7)*
*Wilberfoss CE Primary School*

## SCORCHING SUMMER

Summer is a bright, light month,
The sky is blue,
The wind blows high,
Dry plants droop,
The sun is like orange juice,
Grass is bright green,
The leaves are wriggling,
Tree branches are full of birds.

*Sarah Veitch (7)*
*Wilberfoss CE Primary School*

## LOVE

Love is yellow,
It smells like chocolate,
It tastes like nice toffee,
It sounds like groovy music,
It feels like soft, loving animals,
It lives in the air and floats down to everyone around it.

*Nikol Bishell-Wells (9)*
*Wilberfoss CE Primary School*

## AUTUMN DAYS

Another season,
A*U*tumn days,
Harves*T*'s growing still,
*U*nderneath the rain they play,
*M*ornings are darkening,
Wi*Nter* comes once again.

*Georgina Pattison (10)*
*Wilberfoss CE Primary School*

## WICKED WINTER

Windy weather, snow and hail,
I really like it when I see Jack Frost.
Slippery ice when I am ice skating,
Very cold playing snowball fights.
Damp and horrid wet weather
When I play out with my friends.
The rain begins to fall.
I go inside to have a drink.
It is very warm inside the house.
Then a snowstorm began to fall,
I got under my bed covers.
I went to sleep,
For once, for all.

*Daniel Poole (7)*
*Wilberfoss CE Primary School*


## JACK FROST LAST NIGHT

Snow and ice from Jack Frost last night,
Ice on the pond sparkly bright.
Throwing snowballs at my little sister,
Making her cry,
My mum hugged and kissed her.
Opening presents on Christmas Day,
A present for the horse, that's only hay.
Ice skating on the pond,
My sister can't she's only one.
My sister fell over and she cried,
She said she nearly died - but she didn't.

*Hannah Green (8)*
*Wilberfoss CE Primary School*

## SCHOOL

Wakey, wakey, rise and shine,
Oh no it's quarter to nine!
Dad's at work, Mum's in bed,
Deary me I haven't read!

First is art, best of all,
Music lesson in the hall.
Bell for lunch very loud,
Out in playground what a crowd.

Now it's time for tables test,
I think I've tried my very best.
Next is science, very boring,
All the kids are loudly snoring.

Bell has rung, end of day,
All the kids scurry away.

*Francesca Bennet (10)*
*Wilberfoss CE Primary School*


## A FROSTY DAY

In winter you go outside,
Play in the snow, you go under a tree,
Cold winter snow falls on you.
Call on your friends, throw snowballs at you,
Build a snowman if you're lucky.
Snowflakes fall silently,
Get your sledge out and skid
Around on the freezing snow,
See who can stay on the blue, fast sledge the longest.

*Harry Hughes (7)*
*Wilberfoss CE Primary School*

## THE FLOOD

I can break angrily through doors,
    And climb up winding stairs.
I can violently charge through fields,
    And gush down streets.

I can destroy houses and gardens,
    And drown families with my raging waves.
I can slip slyly over pavements,
    And silently slide through cracks.

I can wreck boats and ships,
    And break loving hearts.
I can shatter schools,
    And destroy woodlands and farms.

But when my work is done,
    I return to my home, the sea.

*Katherine Ames-Ettridge (10)*
*Wilberfoss CE Primary School*


## SUMMER IN THE GARDEN

It was the last day of spring,
The nights were getting warm,
Sunrise and morning came.
I got dressed,
And went outside, it was scorching hot.
Outside I made a picnic,
The grass was hot,
Petals from plants feel hot like a kettle boiling,
Trees were green like the grass,
The sky was blue.

*Elliot Etherington (7)*
*Wilberfoss CE Primary School*

## LURING MAIDENS

Three maidens lost on an island far
From the civilised world and ways,
Where no sane persons dwell,
On the sea-worn island's bays.

Many a battered broken wreck
Rests on the Isle of Doom,
Lured by the mutant's power
Into the depths of gloom.

Many a man hath lost his life
To the maidens and their evil quest,
To destroy for eternity
All sailors sailing smoothly west.

No one has survived
To tell of the dreadful fate,
Of the forsaken sailors
And the terror evil can create.

*Alice Bean (11)*
*Wilberfoss CE Primary School*


## SUN IN THE GARDEN

It was summer
And I was playing in the garden.
Looking up I saw the sky,
It was bright blue like our blue school jumpers.
I went on my slide and it was hot,
So was the weather.
Suddenly I saw some flowers blooming,
There were daffodils, daises and lupins.

*Esme Dawber (7)*
*Wilberfoss CE Primary School*

## SCHOOL DAY

School is open late today,
Cloudy skies are turning grey,
Lost my jumper, what a day,
The sun is shining, hip, hip hooray.

Maths is boring, can't stop snoring,
Bell has rung,
I feel so young,
Inside play, outside it's pouring.

PE, tripped on tiles, fell in pool,
I've never felt such a fool.
Children playing, truth or dare,
It really, really was not fair.

Time for lunch, it was mouldy bread,
And chicken leg,
I cracked my fingers in the hall,
I went to sit next to Paul.

*Rachael Cotgrave (11)*
*Wilberfoss CE Primary School*


## WINTER DAYS

Winter weather is very white with cloudy snow.
Hailstones fall fast like lots of people in a massive run.
Everyone wears gloves and hats.
Fingers and toes tingle.
Children skate on ice.
I see my breath like grey smoke,
Then it springs back.

*Rosie Bentley (8)*
*Wilberfoss CE Primary School*

## INSIDE MY HEAD

Inside my head there's a washing machine,
To wash all my thoughts away.

Inside my head there's a chocolate river,
To rinse my head out.

Inside my head there's a big calendar,
To give me all my dates.

Inside my head there's a large TV,
Where all my stories are played.

Inside my head there's a pit,
For all my bad memories.

Inside my head there's a filing cabinet,
Where all the things I learn is put.

Inside my head there's a calculator,
To add up numbers.

Inside my head there's a CD player,
To play all my favourite music.

Inside my head,
There's everything I need.

*Katie Last (9)*
*Wilberfoss CE Primary School*


## IN THE SCORCHING SUMMER

In summer it's scorching hot,
People are sweaty.
The sky is light blue,
Not a cloud in it.
People go out to play.

Little children want their paddling pools.
Mums say alright.
Flowers go droopy
Like they are sad.
Mums are sunbathing in the hot day.

*Serena Leach (7)*
*Wilberfoss CE Primary School*


## SCHOOL SUCKS

Gotta get up, late again,
School's open, where's my pen?
Yelled Mum, where's my breakfast?
Better hurry or I'll be last!

Oh phew, just in time,
I sat down and did a class rhyme.
Oh no, a spelling test,
I don't think I did my best!

Science started, someone farted,
Gas explosion, people parted.
Times tables, not so bad,
Then I saw a handsome lad!

School is over, hip, hip hooray!
I wish I was going on holiday.
Put my feet up, watch TV,
Fell asleep, dreamed of the sea.

Got woken up my mum,
Then I kicked her up the bum.
Yippee! Bangers and mash for tea,
There's nothing better than that for me!

*Robyn Childe (10)*
*Wilberfoss CE Primary School*

## THE FLOOD

I can
Stir from my bed sleepily in the
Early hours of the morning,
Yawn, stretch and groan.

I can
Slyly tear into houses when nobody's home,
Crashing, smashing, wrecking.

I can
Get into rooms without a key,
Swiftly, rapidly and nimbly.

I can
Get out of the house with
Care, caution and wariness.

I can
Slide gracefully through the forest
To my true home,
The sea.

*Amy Gover (11)*
*Wilberfoss CE Primary School*


## SPRING GARDEN

One spring morning I saw plants covering the plant bed,
Flowers sprouting like puddles getting larger and longer,
Raining like tears coming from an eye.
It was a cool breeze
Like a pale blue sky,
With the wind blowing the clouds.

*Katrina Graves (8)*
*Wilberfoss CE Primary School*

## THE FLOOD

I'm on my way to destroy more land,
I wish and whirl like a crying child bawling and biting.
I feel angry and cross, so cross that I force down doors with my power.
I live to harm!
I make trouble without any problem,
I terrorise people in the streets,
I'm like a mini whirlpool sucking things in with my willpower.
I swish and scream at anyone or thing that survives.
I break into banks, and wreck the bridges,
I'm the king of the land.
I rule this world.
I harm things proudly,
And then I slowly drift back to the calming riverbed.

*Alice Sey (10)*
*Wilberfoss CE Primary School*


## THE FLOOD

I can twist and swerve and knock over cars.
When I'm angry I can wickedly flood everywhere.

I can flood the fields with a gigantic big roar.
I can fly through windows and shoot under doors.

I can creep into beds and slither into pillows.
I like to sternly go into schools and shops and torture everybody.

I can go everywhere in houses, make doors slam and go upstairs.
I bashfully knock walls down and run into castles.

*Jake Gilbertson (11)*
*Wilberfoss CE Primary School*

## COLD WINTER

In winter it is very cold,
Icy and slippery.
When it is cold Jack Frost
Comes out at night.
In the morning you breathe lightly,
You can see your breath.
Hailstones are heavy
In winter when it is cold
Thick white snow is very cold.
The children put on hats and gloves.
In winter the wind blows
And makes me shiver.

*Rachel Hopwood (8)*
*Wilberfoss CE Primary School*


## A GREAT WINTER

Winter is cold,
As cold as a mountain,
When it snows white and blowy
The wind blows like someone smoking,
It snows like tiny soft clouds,
When a snowflake touches me
It melts and says goodbye,
The snowflakes are glorious,
As glorious as can be,
Everybody runs to shelter
Under a tree or a snow covered wooden hut.

*Rebecca Bowe (7)*
*Wilberfoss CE Primary School*

## FLOOD

I can glide down the streets
And up hills,
I can smash open doors,
I can badly shatter windows,
I can knock down the living
And viciously drown creatures,
I can slyly sneak through cracks in walls
And trash schools,
I destroy people's relatives
And I don't care,
I kill the living and wash away the dead,
Then I return to my home feeling very happy.

I am very unpleasant.

*Josh Barrett (10)*
*Wilberfoss CE Primary School*


## GOLD

Gleaming brightly now the sun
Climbs golden skies, night is done
Watching over golden lands
Orange seas and golden sands.
Swaying in the autumn breeze
Skeleton plants, losing leaves
Golden fields hold golden corn
Dewdrops glisten in the morn
Golden mice scamper about
Under gold grasses they peep out
Lazy goldfish swim the streams
Cockerels calling midst a dream.

*Catriona Burns (10)*
*Wilberfoss CE Primary School*

## I Want To Be A ...

I'd like to be a footballer,
I can run really fast.
I'd like to be a footballer
Like the stars from the past.

I'd like to be a cricketer,
I can hit balls really far.
I'd like to be a cricketer,
I'm a batting, bowling star.

I'd like to be a racing driver,
I can speed round the track.
I'd like to be a racing driver
Always looking forward, never looking back.

*Alex Nattrass (8)*
*Wilberfoss CE Primary School*


## In Winter Land

In winter it snows,
And also has got a wintry breeze,
It blows and blows like Santa Claus breathing.
It's freezing and icy, the water goes hard,
And it stand there as hard as a rock,
And as still as a wall.
There are no leaves on the trees,
The windy breeze blows them off.
Breath comes out of my mouth like I'm smoking.

*Rachel Hudson (7)*
*Wilberfoss CE Primary School*

## MY DOG

I really love my dog,
She is called Holly,
She's cute and cuddly, hardly ever bites,
And she's as greedy as a hog.

We bought her when she was a puppy,
Small, cute and gold,
She was the first pet we ever had,
And so sweet to hold.

She's getting older and older,
But it doesn't show,
She's always happy and bouncy,
I love her loads and loads.

*Zoe Robinson (9)*
*Wilberfoss CE Primary School*


## AUTUMN

Golds, browns and greens
Fall carelessly through the scenes.
As we cut through unruly brambles
The helpless hedgehog carefully ambles.
Round and round swirls the leaf
Falling from the adventurous tree,
That always weaves.
As all the flowers wilt,
They make a pattern like a quilt.

*Victoria Gomersall (10)*
*Wilberfoss CE Primary School*

## SCHOOL DAY

School is open, late again,
Gotta get up, grab my pen,
A maths lesson at half-past ten,
Oops I forgot to feed the hen.

People running, people shouting,
I can't wait for the school outing.
Lost my socks, lost my shoes,
In football I always lose.

There's the bell,
Got to go,
School is over,
Oh no, I've forgotten my bag.

*David Laverack (10)*
*Wilberfoss CE Primary School*


## SCHOOL TIME!

School is open, late again!
I have no ink in my pen,
To assembly, say amen,
Now a maths test, at half-past ten.

Break is here, no need to fear,
I've got to get into gear,
The loud school bell is ringing,
Now for lots of dreadful singing.

My singing voice is very bad,
My friends think I'm very mad,
Times tables again,
Got them wrong, all the shame.

*Samuel Vale (10)*
*Wilberfoss CE Primary School*

## WHAT A DAY

Early morning, maths again,
Head is hurting, oh the pain.
Teacher asking questions hard!
Time for playing in the yard.

Lunchtime started, people bunch,
Boy I'm glad that I'm packed lunch!
Later on, double English,
I sneakily chomp on sticky liquorice.

Time for test in IT,
Lost my map in geography,
We all start yelling, hip, hip, hooray!
For the bell has gone, what a day!

*Katie Bentley (11)*
*Wilberfoss CE Primary School*


## FLOOD

I can smash doors down and ransack houses,
And destroy memories.
I can crush trees violently,
I am never happy.

I angrily destroy roads,
I destroy anything in my path,
No one gets in my way,
I destroy land.

I can flood everywhere,
I can run up the stairs,
And flood a whole house.

*Ashley Oliver-Scott (10)*
*Wilberfoss CE Primary School*

## SCHOOL DAY

Got to get up, feed the hens,
Grabbed my bag, grabbed my pens,
Met my friends, on the way to school,
They really think, they are so cool.

Wrote a story, page of sums,
Met worst enemy, she said I was dumb.
PE now, time to dance,
Time to jump, space to prance.

It's not so bad, just so dim,
Read class novel, sang a hymn.
Trip day, lots of rules,
Tripped up, looked a fool.

Did some science, lots of graphing,
Answered questions, day of dafting.
Bell rings, on our way,
School forgotten, till next day.

*Zoe Frost (11)*
*Wilberfoss CE Primary School*


## THE FLOOD

I can sprint onto road, past lots of houses,
I can slide under doorways, fill up a room,
And toss stuff about, I destroy all houses,
I slither around in a rage, no one can take me away,
I will not stop.

I will leave this land and go back to my home, the sea
To destroy more innocents lands, you just wait.

*Joseph Mellanby (11)*
*Wilberfoss CE Primary School*

## BIRTHDAYS

Birthdays are so special,
They're lots and lots of fun.
Jelly, ice cream, birthday cake
And a chocolate bun.

Early in the morning
Arrives the postman,
The envelopes go
Bang! Bang! Bang!

Lots of lovely cards inside
From everyone I know.
Put them on the mantelpiece
Neatly in a row.

Beautifully wrapped presents,
Tear the paper open wide.
It's so exciting
To find out what's inside.

Banners and balloons
To decorate the room.
Enjoy the party music,
Boom! Boom! Boom!

Birthdays are so special,
They're lots and lots of fun,
With lots of happy memories
When the day is done.

*Jessica Fleming (8)*
*Wilberfoss CE Primary School*

## A Riddle

A car carrier,
A boat barrier.

A gravel wearer,
A tyre bearer.

A great gripper,
A sly slipper.

All this to make me
A road!

*Matthew Poole (10)*
*Wilberfoss CE Primary School*


## A?

A sly slitherer,
A blood shiverer.

A flicking tail,
A spitting male.

A vicious biter,
A hissing fighter.

A catalogue to make me a snake.

*Caroline Harrow (10)*
*Wilberfoss CE Primary School*


## The World

The world is beyond me,
It is all around,
The world is very strange,
It makes very funny sounds.

My life is beyond me,
It stretches out wide,
There's lots of people in the world,
But my mum will always be by my side.

*Lois Gilbertson (9)*
*Wilberfoss CE Primary School*

## A KENNING

A venom spitter,
A sly hitter.

A hard biter,
A good fighter.

A smooth slider,
A crafty hider.

A catalogue to make me a cobra.

*Mark Cundle (9)*
*Wilberfoss CE Primary School*

## MY DOG

My dog is nice and furry,
He's cute and cuddly and barks at everyone.

He chases cats and birds, day and night.

My dog is cool and that's what I like.

My dog is sweet and neat.

*Rachel Alexander-Pratt (9)*
*Wilberfoss CE Primary School*

## My School Day

School is open, late *again!*
Not done my homework, lost my pen!
First assembly, sat next to Jim,
Chris got a telling from Mrs Simm!

Next a maths test, what a bore!
I bet I get the lowest score!
Then it is lunchtime, roast pork and chips,
Soggy crackers and cheesy dips!

Licked the spoon, in chemistry
Nearly exploded! Silly me!
The bell has gone, hip, hip, hooray!
No more school for another day!

*Rebecca McFetridge (10)*
*Wilberfoss CE Primary School*


## Autumn

Autumn's dawning,
Autumn's gaining,
Autumn's coming,
Autumn's nearly here.
Leaves are going brown and crumply
And you fall fast asleep
Autumn's looking through your windows
Which must mean autumn's here.

*Sophie Ollerenshaw (9)*
*Wilberfoss CE Primary School*

### Farmer Joe Had A Pig

Farmer Joe had a pig,
It loved to dress up wearing a wig,
It was blue and pink,
The other pigs gave it a wink,
It was so proud of its looks,
It read the latest fashion books,
Green and yellow shoes it had,
But Farmer Joe thought it was mad,
Purple and orange trousers it wore,
The other pigs couldn't believe what they saw,
Red spotty shirt,
Never went near any dirt,
Turquoise striped coat,
Off it goes on a boat,
Guess why it was all dressed up?
It was going on a date!

*Emily Childe (9)*
*Wilberfoss CE Primary School*


### Parents

Parents, parents, they're always at work,
It always makes me go berserk.
Parents, parents, they're rubbish at art,
I would rather paint a jam tart.
Parents, parents, they can't make my bed,
I have lost my head.
Parents, parents, they pretend to be sick,
They think we are so thick.

*James Hopwood (10)*
*Wilberfoss CE Primary School*

## FUTURE

Future is the world ahead,
It's past floating away.
Future is advance technology,
It's past melted history.
Future is people at old age,
It's past going into books.
Future is charity raising,
It's past many years below.
Future is school at home,
It's past thrown in the bin.
Future is years in front,
It's past just being forgotten.
Future is more money,
It's past as poor as can be.
Future is what we want!

*Alex Gurnell (9)*
*Wilberfoss CE Primary School*


## GOLF

Golf is really wicked,
I play it every day.
I hit the ball into the hedge,
And never get it back.
My neighbour gets really angry,
He shouts out from next door,
Tells me off for smashing a window
And says he'll tell my mum.
My mum will ground me for a week,
I'd better keep quiet and not give cheek.

*Jason Nattrass (8)*
*Wilberfoss CE Primary School*

## THE SUN

The sun is a golden yellow,
it sparkles in the sky.
It gleams throughout the day
and all over the sky.
The sun is a rainbow of gold,
sitting in the sky,
we don't want the sun to die.
The sun puts you out of your miseries,
it puts your hopes high.
The sun is a golden wafer
sitting in the sky,
it brightens up the world
each and every day.
The sun is a yummy golden bun
it's so untouchable and to hot to try.

*Andreas Symeonides (10)*
*Wilberfoss CE Primary School*


## THE MAGIC BOX

In my magic box I see
Question marks and exclamation marks
Fighting with each other,
And buildings standing proud in the noisy cities.
In my magic box I see
Trees whistling wistfully,
I also see the sun in a good morning mood,
And then the moon rises gladly stretching his arms.

*Christopher Fenn (10)*
*Wilberfoss CE Primary School*

## LIFE!

Life can be like a thunderstorm
Or a tornado in a spin.
You need to learn the rules of life
And hold them tight within.

L   earn in your life and be wise.
I    n everything always be true.
F   riends will be the prize.
E   verything will come to you.

My life is like a ray of sunshine,
Or a dark, empty room.

What is your life like?

*Ryan Downes (9)*
*Wilberfoss CE Primary School*


## MOBILE PHONES

When I get a mobile phone
I'll always want the best tone,
That's what I want when I get a phone.

When I get a phone
I'll text all night,
And try not to cause a fight,
That's what I'll do when I get a phone.

When I get a phone
I'll ring all day,
Then I'll go out for a play,
That's what I'll do when I get a phone.

*Tom Connell (9)*
*Wilberfoss CE Primary School*

## FUN IN THE SNOW

I like skiing in the snow,
Boots on, skis down and off I go.
Past the snowy trees, I feel an icy breeze,
Snowflakes on my nose, makes me want to sneeze!

Down I go, down I go, down the mountainside,
It's like a gigantic snowy slide.
Push and glide, I know how
To stop, I do the snow plough.

The chair lift takes me back to the top,
Then I jump off with a great big hop!
Down I go, down and down again,
Then back to the top and start again!

*Jemma Bayes (9)*
*Wilberfoss CE Primary School*


## FIREWORKS

Flickering, spitting, squeaking, shooting fireworks
Blowing red, green, yellow, blue and pink.
Bang, boom, like the Second World War,
Bang over there, now over here!
It's OK watching but sleeping!
Spitting, spreading, when will it end?
Red, green, blue, yellow, pretty.
Pitter-patter, pitter-patter, rain, rain, rain!
Coming spitting on the burning fire,
Shadowing, shadowing, sinking to the ground.

*Tom Hughes (9)*
*Wilberfoss CE Primary School*

## GOING TO A THEME PARK

Going to a theme park on a sunny day,
When you see all the rides that you've got to play
As you jump up and say,
'I need some money to make something out of the day,
As it is my birthday in May,
I've got to have a twenty pound note.'
Queuing for the roller coaster, jumping all about,
Whizzing down the roller coaster, the wind in your ears.
Sitting in the relaxing place drinking lots of beers,
Relaxing in a boat with a cool drink of cola,
As you realise you're going nowhere you jump up and start to row.
When you get to the exit you look back
And repeat in your mind how fantastic the day was.

*Ashley Cattle  (8)*
*Wilberfoss CE Primary School*


## THE ROLY-POLY BIRD

Deep in the forest
Up in the trees,
Was the roly-poly bird
Flying in the breeze.
He flew up high,
He flew down low,
Don't ask me why
Cos I don't know.
His feathers were bright,
The colours just stand out,
As he takes off to flight
All the animals shout.

*Alice Ames Ettridge  (8)*
*Wilberfoss CE Primary School*

## TEACHERS

Teachers are bossy, weird and fat
They make you think that you're a rat.
They don't know when you're muddled or stuck
They might even swallow you up.
They don't care if you're not at school
They probably say hip, hip hooray.
They run and chase you with a broom
They shout and scream and screech till noon.
They don't know how to do mathematics or science
They can't even write properly.
They wear their glasses back to front
Now how silly is that?
They make you clean the cupboards and dust the walls
Even though they are clean
But that's the school rule.

*Jade Taylor (10)*
*Wilberfoss CE Primary School*


## SCHOOL

School is fun,
School is hard.
The school teachers are strict, but good at art,
The maths is great,
The school dinners are alright,
And me and my friends never fight.
PE is the best cos it's fun,
And my favourite book is 'Dancing in the sun'.
We start at nine,
And leave at twenty five to four.

*Jade Watson (9)*
*Wilberfoss CE Primary School*

## SEASONS

S ummer is a time for hot summer weather,
U sually we have ice cream and a family barbecue.
M y best friend Sam is a size five shoe which is quite funny!
M y mum likes sitting outside sunbathing with her best friend.
E veryday is scorching. I don't even think we are in England.
R azing hot it really is.

*Elliott Murphy (10)*
*Wilberfoss CE Primary School*


## JOKER

J ames the Joker, a powerful card,
O ver the top, the king and queen's guard,
K icking its way through the invisible air,
E rmine clothing over his hair,
R avenous, stealthy and a crazy guy,
S tarting crimes in the blink of an eye.

*Lawrence Crawford (10)*
*Wilberfoss CE Primary School*


## SWEETS

S weets are nice and tasty
W e like to scoff them too
E ating and eating, we like that most
E very Friday night we eat lots and lots
T asty Tic Tacs and little goodies
S pecial treats from Mum and Dad.

*Sarah Hartas (10)*
*Wilberfoss CE Primary School*

## CHLOE

Black and white, big bright eyes, big floppy ears.
Long, soft fur until she was clipped for the summer.
She was always there, we grew up together, like sisters.
Paw on my hand for attention,
Howling happy birthday at my parties.
Whining at my door, jumping on my bed,
Begging for my biscuits, she always got some.
Walking on the lead, running on the lead.
Let off in the woods. Excited.
Running, chasing stones, running round in circles, tripping me up.
Big silver bowl full of dried food, crunching in my ear.
Picking up food we have dropped.
No more whining at my door. No more crunching dried food,
No more barking when I get home. No more kisses.
No more suffering for Chloe.

*Emma Knutton  (10)*
*Wilberfoss CE Primary School*


## HENRY MY DOG

Henry our dog is really cool
You sit on the sofa
And he jumps up on top of you!
When Dad has his shoes on
He dances and jumps.
He slobbers all over you
And scratches his ears
But we love him loads.

*Amanda Smillie  (10)*
*Wilberfoss CE Primary School*

## MASH POTATO

Mash potato is so lumpy,
My mum makes it so bumpy.
Even though it is potato
It's still so lumpy,
But this time it is not even bumpy,
And now it is not even lumpy,
My mum has finally mashed it properly.

*Robert Pickard (8)*
*Wilberfoss CE Primary School*


## MY SENSES

I like to watch
people playing rugby
and dogs run about in the park.

I like to listen
to the buzz of the fridge
and the bark of the dog.

I like the smell
of warm apple pie
and a burning fire.

I like the taste
of apple pie
and Yorkshire puddings.

I like the feel
of my teddy bears
and the smoothness of my hair.

*Rory Megginson (8)*
*Woodfield Community Primary School*

## I SENSE

I like to hear the sound
of the whistling wind
sneaking down chimneys
trying to blow out
the dazzling warm fire,
spiders scurrying along
the squeaky floorboards
making webs in dark corners.

My senses help me
to survive and they
keep me alive.

I like to taste the juicy pears
as they slip and slide
in my mouth,
the crunchy biscuits that
immediately break into crumbs.

My senses help me
to survive and they
keep me alive.

I like to watch
the birds flutter in
all directions like a parade,
the bright colours of a circus
with clowns dancing
and performing.

My senses help me
to survive and they
keep me alive.

*Andrew Lewis (9)*
*Woodfield Community Primary School*

## PERFORMANCE POETRY

I like to watch
My friends play happily together.
The amazing stars sparkle merrily
And the moon grinning cheesily at the enormous world.

I like to listen
To people laughing in the wonderful world.
The trees swaying in the cold, icy wind
And the nightingale singing her delightful song.

I like the smell
Of honeysuckle and roses.
Tea bubbling in the oven
And coffee in the teapot.

I like the taste
Of ice cream melting creamily in your mouth.
Greasy, slippy chicken skin tip from one side to the other
And chocolate sauce trickling down my tongue.

I like the feel
Of fluffy warm kittens.
Warm, cosy mittens
And woolly school jumpers.

*Sasha Buck (8)*
*Woodfield Community Primary School*

## PERFORMANCE POETRY

I like to watch
My cat stalk along the colourful fence,
Then she leaps down to the field
And finds her other cat friends.

I like to listen
To the loud TV downstairs when I go to my cosy warm bed
And the bath running in the morning.
The people shouting and laughing when I come to school
And the teachers explaining our work.

I like to smell
Chicken cooking in honey sauce.
Fresh air when I go outside.

I like the taste
Of pepperoni pizza hot in my mouth.
Salt and vinegar crisps dissolving when I eat,
Crunchy, sweet, chewy and soft.

I like to feel
My cat's fur when I stroke her,
My mum cuddling me,
The breeze on my face.

*Ian Porter (8)*
*Woodfield Community Primary School*

## SENSING MY WORLD

I like to watch
an arch of a rainbow.
I like to watch
a wave of grass wobbling in the wind.
1, 2, 3, 4, I use my senses to learn more.
I like to watch
trampolining hailstones, bouncing on the rooftops.
I like to watch
the lightning, ripping the skies apart.
1, 2, 3, 4, I use my senses to learn more.
I like to watch
wobbling jelly on a plate.
I like to watch birds peck the soil for worms.
1, 2, 3, 4, I use my senses to learn more.

*Matthew Button (8)*
*Woodfield Community Primary School*


## THOMAS

I like to watch
my parakeet play loudly in his big cage.

I like to listen
to my mum make big, fat chocolate cakes
with eggs on top.

I like the smell
of hot Ribena.

I like the touch
of my soft cat on the back.

*Thomas Claxton (9)*
*Woodfield Community Primary School*

## SENSING MY WORLD

I like to see the rain
rushing like a waterfall
coming down the windowpane.
I like to see ice
like witches fingers
on the trees.

My senses keep me alive
and they help me to survive.

I like to hear
wind roaring
like a lion.
I like to hear wolves rumbling
like an engine.

*Emily Rowe (9)*
*Woodfield Community Primary School*


## PERFORMANCE POETRY

I like to look at the bright sun
slowly moving across the sky on a summer's day.

I like to look at the bare trees
swaying in the breeze on a winter day.

I like to look at the snow
gently falling while I sit by the fire.

I like to look at the long trains
pass by as I go over the iron bridge.

I like to look at the sailors
unhook the boats when I go on holiday to Majorca.

*Jack Clayton (9)*
*Woodfield Community Primary School*

## KIRSTY OWEN

There's a famous, posh place called Harrogate,
That's noted for shops and spa water
And Mr and Mrs Owen
Went there with young Kirsty, their daughter.

A fab little girl was young Kirsty,
All dressed in modern, cool clothes,
With accessories such as sunglasses,
But others, like scrunchies she loathes.

They didn't think much to the shops,
The clothes were expensive and dull,
There were no fashion icons or trends
And the restaurants were all full.

So they searched for other cafes,
They paid for coffee and tea,
There they'd got biscuits and fancy cakes,
The town centre was what they could see.

There was a big waitress called Norma,
Who's nose was covered with spots,
She was known to be very clumsy,
With cups, saucers and pots.

Now Kirsty had been talking with family,
How Norma could be so clumsy and fast,
Tripping over a loose floorboard,
She dropped steaming pots as she passed.

So straight away the courageous lass,
Not showing any burning pain,
She rushed to the hospital quick,
And ran through water, frost and rain.

Then Mr and Mrs Owen
Quite rightly complained to the boss
Boss said, 'How much will it cost to pay?'
For their enormous, upsetting loss.

***Bethanie Sturdy, Kirsty Owen (11) & Charlotte Voakes (10)***
***Woodfield Community Primary School***

## WHAT I LIKE

I like to watch
Squirrels jump far from tree to tree,
My cat rattling her teeth hungrily looking at birds,
Rabbits hopping quickly along the grass.

I like to listen
To my cool music,
The radio station 97.2 Stray FM,
My cat purring happily as I run my hand through her fur.

I like the smell
Of my mum's jumper as I give her a non-forgetful hug,
My clean shiny hair,
Tasty pizza.

I like the taste
Of salt and vinegar crisps, nipping my tongue,
Spicy pepperoni pizza,
Soft red tomatoes and cool green cucumber.

I like to feel
My cat's soft fur,
My mum when she hugs me,
My pillow at night,
*Safe.*

***Carlene Smith (9)***
***Woodfield Community Primary School***

## SHAUN DEEMING

There's a famous busy place called Leeds,
That's noted for football and fun
And Mr and Mrs Deeming
Went with young Shaun, their son.

An impressive little lad, was young Shaun,
All dress in his football kit,
With a scarf waves above his head,
The best gear that Allsports could get.

They didn't think much of the football match,
The players, they didn't do scoring,
There were no fouls, or accidents,
Fact, it was getting very boring.

So seeking for further amusements
They paid, and entered the fair,
At that, they went on the well good Ice Blast,
And all three had a seat to share.

There was a bad fault in the seat they sat in,
When the Ice Blast was at full speed,
The seat started to creak and twirl around,
And the father started to plead.

Now, when Shaun fell off he instantly died,
His parents just stood there and stared,
At last they all said, 'That is a shame,
Please manager, what is the fare?'

So while they discussed this situation,
The manager gave them the dosh,
The father grinned as it was placed in his hand,
'With this we'll become quite posh!'

You could not tell that the parents were sad,
'We'll get another boy on loan,
But now dear, we'll just have to do.'
And they both gracefully walked home.

*Alex Lenton (11) & Shaun Deeming (10)*
*Woodfield Community Primary School*


## PERFORMANCE POETRY

I like to watch
The stars twinkle in the night sky,
The lamp shade's light,
The tree's branches swing high in the air.

I like to listen
To the eggs spitting in the pan,
The birds' cheeping in a soft voice,
The rain tapping on the windows.

I like the smell
Of the lemon on the pancakes,
The smell of fresh air outside,
Pizza on the tray.

I like the taste
Of ice cream that melts on my tongue,
The fish fingers from Asda,
The strawberry taste of my mum's trifles.

I like to feel
The breeze on my face,
And the fur on animals
And the bed clothes on my bed.

*Emily Webster (8)*
*Woodfield Community Primary School*

## DANIEL JOHNSON

There's a famous museum called Jorvik,
That's noted for its historical fun
And Mr and Mrs Johnson
Went there with young Daniel, their son.

An active little devil was Daniel,
All dressed in his best, so he thought,
With a catapult that he carried,
It was the best he'd ever bought.

They didn't think much of the history,
The people were totally fake,
They already knew about Vikings,
So why come here, for goodness sake?

So trying to find somewhere else to go,
Took a lot of hard work and thought,
Suddenly they came to a cinema,
'Let's go,' they said, tickets were bought.

There was a whole choice of movies to watch,
They all decided on Chicken Run,
Everyone said it was gonna be good,
They were right . . . it was extra fun.

Now Daniel was starting to get bored,
He thought he would liven it up,
He started searching his pockets
And pulled out his best catapult.

So he loaded it with mud and stones,
And pulled out a steady aim,
He shot it at the cinema screen,
He certainly enjoyed this game.

You could definitely see no one liked it,
The shattered screen on the floor,
Everybody turned round to see him,
They knew it was him for sure.

Then it wasn't long 'til the manager came,
His face was steaming with heat,
And then before Daniel knew it,
They were all chucked out on the street.

***Daniel Johnson (11), Tim Newell & Kelly Gilmour (9)***
***Woodfield Community Primary School***

## SENSING MY WORLD

I like to watch
the snowdrop on the floor,
the sun shine in my window.

I like to listen
to the waves wash and wash,
the people talking in school,
the OHP switching on.

I like to smell
bacon in the morning,
the smell of fire.

I like to touch
my big guinea pig
Plasticine melting.

I like to taste
spaghetti Bolognese,
ice cream melt in my mouth.

***Daniel Andrews-Turner (8)***
***Woodfield Community Primary School***

## LEAH MERCER

There's a famous seaside place called Scarborough,
It's noted for its boats on the water,
And Mr and Mrs Mercer
Went there with Leah, their groovy daughter.

A smart, trendy girl is young Leah,
She always looked neat and smart,
But she had some smelly trainers,
From which she would not part.

The stench from those shoes was appalling,
It made her friends feel really sick,
They begged and they cried and they pleaded,
For her some new trainers to pick.

So they went into town to do shopping,
Some shiny new shoes to be got,
Would they succeed in their mission,
Sadly for noses they did not.

Now, they went home with the smelly trainers,
And cried and they gave a weary sigh,
So Leah went to school with those trainers,
Then Leah's feet went really dry.

*Natalie Healey (10), Hollie Forge & Leah Mercer (9)*
*Woodfield Community Primary School*

## PERFORMANCE POETRY

I like to listen to the sound of the phone ringing downstairs
when no one answers it.
As the night lengthens
the gentle wind as it blows in-between the trees
and the distant motor of a car.

1, 2, 3, 4, 5
my senses have just done a jive.

I like to listen to the tick, tick, tick, tick of my clock.
As the night lengthens
the birds, faraway birds calling to me
and a distant police siren breaks the silence.

1, 2, 3, 4, 5
my senses are alive.

*Kelly McQuigg (9)*
*Woodfield Community Primary School*

## SENSING MY WORLD

I like to watch
The scarlet, red blood drip from a deep cut,
Children laughing in the park,
The stars glittering in the night sky.

I like to listen
To the buzzing of a bee,
Noises here and there,
Clashing of knives and forks at tea,
The growling of a bear.

I like the smell
Of chicken with curry sauce,
Fresh air when I go outside,
Air freshener when it is sprayed.

I like the taste
Of ice cream so sweet,
Chocolate melting so creamy in your mouth.

I like to feel
Cold chills running up my spine,
The ice cream in my mouth.

*Natalie Robinson-Bramley (8)*
*Woodfield Community Primary School*

## SENSES

I like to listen to the sound of the TV humming softly,
as the night lengthens,
the quiet rustling of my hamster
as she moves her bedding about,
a distant car horn tooting,
the quiet chatting of Mum and Dad
as they have their tea.

Ears and eyes keep my senses alive,
but nose and tongue are best.

I like to listen to the small sound of my brother
tapping at keys on his computer,
as the night lengthens,
the scary sound of the wind howling,
a distant rattle of the windowpane,
the faraway sound of dogs
ferociously barking in their fight for food.

Ears and eyes keep my senses alive,
but nose and tongue are best.

*Emma Buckee (8)*
*Woodfield Community Primary School*


## YOUNG HARRY

There's a famous tennis park in Ripon,
That's known as the place for fun,
And Mr and Mrs Teggin
Went there with young Harry, their son.

A very cool lad was young Harry,
All dressed up ready for sport,
With racquet, ball and trainers,
He looked like Tim Henman on court.

He didn't think much of the players,
Their ball skills weren't good at all,
There were volleys, backhands and laughter,
But nothing could make young Harry fall.

So seeking for many more victories,
He went up and played a pro,
Harry got hit really hard by the ball,
His head swelled as he started to fall.

*Mark Teggin, Michael Groves (10) & Billy Wood (9)*
*Woodfield Community Primary School*


## LIGHTWATER VALLEY

There's a great place called Lightwater Valley,
That's famous for danger, for fun,
Our Sarah and our Nick and Luke
Decided to go for a run.

Our fab group of friends with their doodles,
Eventually went on a ride,
But our oldest, Sarah, bright and cool,
Became frightened and went away to hide.

They did not like the look of the ghost train,
It scared them right down to their socks,
They could hear the frightening noises,
And things that jump out of a box.

They like the sticky toffee apples,
That made them dribble and pant,
They bought some and ate them all up,
So they all started to sing and chant.

*Luke Foggin, Sarah Jenner (10) & Nicola Evers (9)*
*Woodfield Community Primary School*

## MY SENSES

I like to listen to the sound
of the choir's soft voices
in the harvest festival.

Hearing, looking, tasting, touching
with all my senses I explore.

I like to listen to the sound
of horses hooves
like someone drumming
in a rock band.

Hearing, looking, tasting, touching
with all my senses I explore.

I like to listen to the crackle, pop
of party poppers
in the celebration of Christmas.

Hearing, looking, tasting, touching
with all my senses I explore.

I like to listen to the flames
flicker and dance
like rustling leaves,
the sound of a train
like a low aeroplane
roar its engine.

Hearing, looking, tasting, touching
with all my senses I explore.

*Lorraine Mazza (8)*
*Woodfield Community Primary School*

## THOMAS STEVENTON

There's a famous old town called Knaresborough,
    That's noted for its age and fun,
And Mr and Mrs Steventon
    Went there with young Thomas, their son.

A bright young chap was Thomas,
    In his Adidas gear, he looked great,
He walked round the shops and the castle,
    He didn't know what was to be his fate.

They didn't think much of the town square,
    The streets were dirty and small,
In the river just nobody drowned,
    Fact, nothing to laugh at all.

So they found something else to do,
    They paid and went to the castle,
Where there were dungeons and gremlins,
    Where Thomas caused a lot of hassle.

There were this one great big 'ole in the floor,
    Which young Thomas fell down quite fast,
And landed in an awkward position,
    And he soon knew he wouldn't last.

Now Thomas started to tunnel out,
    As such a brave young boy was he,
He said, 'I've got such a bad headache,'
    And he died, unfortunately.

*Jonathan Binns (11), Thomas Steventon (10)*
*& George Morton (9)*
*Woodfield Community Primary School*

## Amber

There's a famous, fun place called Flamingo,
That's noted for slides with water
And Mr and Mrs Mazza
Went there with young Amber, their daughter.

A cool little lass was young Amber,
Dressed up in her best jeans which were blue,
With a stick of candyfloss in her hand,
The finest the fun place could do!

While Amber was riding the big wheel,
A seagull flew over her head,
It spotted our beautiful Amber,
And decided to sit there instead.

So when Amber got off the big wheel,
She started to feel very dizzy,
Then she tripped and fell and hurt her knee,
Her mum had a drink that was fizzy.

Now Amber knew a lot about seagulls,
Because she studied them at school,
Everybody in her class liked seagulls,
Pupils think they are very cool.

So a flock of seagulls took her away,
The seagulls took her to a beach,
Amber lay on the really soft sand,
Then the seagulls got Amber a peach.

*Damien Oliver (10) & Jade Moffatt (9)*
*Woodfield Community Primary School*

## TASTE, TOUCH, HEAR AND SEE

I like the sound of bumblebees humming in a tree
I like the sound of rain pattering down on me.

My senses help keep me alive
they help me touch, taste and see,
every day I'm alive they sense the world with me.

I like to see the playful kitten, the one who lives next door
I like to watch the scurrying rabbits munch a mouldy apple core.

My senses help keep me alive
they help me touch, taste and see,
every day I'm alive they sense the world with me.

I like to feel the soft, grey fur on my cat Suzie's belly,
I like to feel the runny juice all around the jelly.

My senses help keep me alive
they help me touch, taste and see,
every day I'm alive they sense the world with me.

*Bethany Aitken (8)*
*Woodfield Community Primary School*